DAY BY DAY

DAY BY DAY
The Notre Dame
Prayerbook for Students

Edited by

THOMAS McNALLY, C.S.C.
Associate Director of Campus Ministry
University of Notre Dame

and

WILLIAM G. STOREY, D.M.S.
Director, Graduate Program in
Liturgical Studies
University of Notre Dame

AVE MARIA PRESS
Notre Dame, Indiana 46556

Acknowledgments:

American Bible Society. Today's English Version of *The Psalms for Modern Man,* © 1970. For Psalms 8, 19, 22, 23, 51, 100, 113, 121, 127, 130, 134, 138, 139, 141, 145, 148, 150.

Darton, Longman & Todd, and Doubleday & Co., Inc. *The Jerusalem Bible,* © 1966. For 14 short New Testament readings.

International Committee on English in the Liturgy, © 1974. For excerpts from the Rite of Penance.

International Consultation on English Texts, © 1970. For Canticle of the Blessed Virgin Mary, Canticle of Zachary, Te Deum, The Apostles' Creed.

Nihil Obstat: Rev. Monsignor Leo A. Hoffmann
              Censor Deputatus

Imprimatur: ✠ Leo A. Pursley
             Bishop of Fort Wayne-South Bend

ISBN 0-87793-100-3

CONTENTS

PREFACE

"Lord, teach us to pray, just as John taught his disciples" (Lk 11:1).

The disciples were the first followers of Jesus to make this request, but not the last. Since apostolic times, Christians have sought ways to deepen their prayer life and come into contact more fully with Jesus and his Father.

I find this true among young persons I encounter—a hunger for prayer often coupled with feelings of dissatisfaction with their present prayer life. Rather than try to answer this yearning with a treatise on the intricacies of prayer, the authors instead present a prayerbook for students.

8

Prayer has many dimensions, many styles, many levels. The selection of prayers and devotions in this book is designed to help young persons expand their consciousness in regard to prayer. By reading and reflecting on the examples, they hopefully will find their prayer life strengthened and their ability to pray facilitated.

Finally, I note that this book revives a proud tradition—the Notre Dame Prayerbook. For years there was a handy-size little prayerbook available in large supply in chapels and chaplain offices on the Notre Dame campus. But styles in prayer change and the book, once so plentiful, is found now in the archives. May this new Notre Dame Prayerbook, so different in contents and appearance, serve the present generation here and elsewhere as well as its predecessor served students of bygone years!

Theodore M. Hesburgh, C.S.C.
President, University of Notre Dame

INTRODUCTION

A prayerbook for students. To some people the idea might sound strange. When they think of students, the word "prayer" does not leap to their lips! But they are wrong.

Our experience with young persons convinces us that many students have the same yearning as those early disciples who asked Jesus to teach them how to pray. Bombarded by expectations and demands from every quarter, and painfully aware of their own confusion and self-doubt, they search for Someone outside themselves.

This is where prayer comes in. It's a hopeful waiting on God, a waiting for someone who does not always show up. A person may feel like the knight in the Bergman movie who says that faith is "like loving someone who is out there in the darkness but never appears, no matter how loudly you call.'' Prayer can be like that.

But sometimes he does show up. He shows us the path, like the headlights on a car which illumine the highway immediately ahead while leaving the rest of the journey in darkness.

To speak about prayer is to speak about waiting. Not only do we wait for God but, in a sense, he waits for us. For reasons fully known by himself alone he decided that we should be free. That means that he obligates himself to wait for us to consent to his coming into our lives.

What if we make ourselves available to him, and he doesn't show up? Should we forget about prayer because we're getting nothing out of it? No. We do not pray to "get something out of it." We pray because we believe he is in our midst, that he is present in the persons and events of our day. By our prayer we recognize his presence and praise his goodness and give thanks for his acts of goodness in our lives. The rest is up to him.

If we pray only when we feel like it we are missing the point of what prayer is. But sometimes prayer is difficult, and hence the need for a book like this. We all need "starters" and "sustainers" from time to time.

To help you pray better, we have drawn on the rich Christian tradition of prayers which have survived the ages. Then we added prayers from our own day as well as prayers from other students who may echo your own doubts and hopes. The book is not meant to be read hurriedly and then placed on a shelf next to *Moby Dick* or *Principles of Calculus*. Keep it handy for reference as your prayer life develops.

Of course, prayer is never easy. At the very least it involves an outlay of time which you have in scarce supply. But, somehow, the efforts, the pain, the struggle all seem worthwhile. This seems to be something Thomas Merton understood very well when he wrote:

> Make ready for the Christ,
> Whose smile, like lightning,
> Sets free the song of everlasting glory
> That now sleeps in your paper flesh,
> Like dynamite.

Thomas McNally, C.S.C.
William G. Storey
University of Notre Dame

I

Prayers for All Seasons

In one way or another, men and women have always prayed. It's part of the human experience. Most prayers are spoken interiorly or aloud and, having performed their task, disappear without a trace. Others find their way into print, and linger.

Of these latter, some have an almost universal appeal. Perhaps we heard them when we were very young, and they stayed with us. Or perhaps we see them for the first time and are jolted at the way they speak to our lives.

Here are samples of what we mean— prayers for all seasons!

DAY BY DAY

Thank you, Lord Jesus Christ,
For all the benefits and blessings
    which you have given me,
For all the pains and insults
    which you have borne for me.
Merciful Friend, Brother and Redeemer,
May I know you more clearly,
Love you more dearly,
And follow you more nearly,
Day by day.

St. Richard of Chichester

GOD BE IN MY HEAD

God be in my head
    and in my understanding.
God be in my eyes
    and in my looking.
God be in my mouth
    and in my speaking.
God be in my heart
    and in my thinking.
God be at my end
    and my departing.

Sarum Primer, 1527

LORD MAKE ME AN INSTRUMENT

Lord, make me an instrument of your peace:
    where there is hatred, let me
        sow love;
    where there is injury, pardon;
    where there is doubt, faith;
    where there is despair, hope;
    where there is darkness, light;
    and where there is sadness, joy.
O Divine Master, grant that I may not so
        much seek
    to be consoled as to console,
    to be understood as to understand,
    to be loved as to love.
For it is in giving that we receive,
    it is in pardoning that we are pardoned,
    and it is in dying that we are born to
        eternal life.

ST. PATRICK'S BREASTPLATE

Christ, be with me, Christ before me, Christ
        behind me,
Christ in me, Christ beneath me, Christ
        above me,
Christ on my right, Christ on my left,
Christ where I lie, Christ where I sit, Christ
        where I arise,
Christ in the heart of every man who thinks
        of me,
Christ in the mouth of every man who
        speaks of me,
Christ in every eye that sees me,
Christ in every ear that hears me.
    Salvation is of the Lord.
    Salvation is of the Lord,
    Salvation is of the Christ.
    May your salvation, O Lord, be ever
        with us.

PRAISES OF GOD

You are holy, Lord, the only God,
    and your deeds are wonderful.
You are strong.
    You are great.
    You are the Most High,
    You are almighty.
    You, holy Father, are
    King of heaven and earth.
You are Three and One,
    Lord God, all good.
    You are Good, all Good, supreme
        Good,
    Lord God, living and true.
You are love,
    You are wisdom.
    You are humility,
    You are endurance.
    You are rest,
    You are peace.
    You are joy and gladness.
    You are justice and moderation.
    You are all our riches,
    And you suffice for us.

You are beauty.
    You are gentleness.
    You are our protector,
    You are our guardian and defender.
    You are courage.
    You are our haven and our hope.
    You are our faith,
        Our great consolation.
        You are our eternal life,
        Great and wonderful Lord,
        God almighty,
        Merciful Savior.

St. Francis of Assisi

AND PEACE AT LAST

May he support us all the day long,
till the shades lengthen
and the evening comes
and the busy world is hushed
and the fever of life is over
and our work is done—
then in his mercy—
may he give us a safe lodging
and a holy rest
and peace at the last.

John Henry Newman

THE ROAD AHEAD

My Lord God,
I have no idea where I am going.
I do not see the road ahead of me.
I cannot know for certain where it will end.
Nor do I really know myself,
and the fact that I think that I am following
    your will does not mean that I am
    actually doing so.
But I believe that the desire to please you
    does in fact please you.
And I hope I have that desire in all that I am
    doing.
I hope that I will never do anything apart
    from that desire.
And I know that if I do this,
you will lead me by the right road though I
    may know nothing about it.
Therefore will I trust you always though I
    may seem to be lost and in the shadow
    of death.
I will not fear, for you are ever with me,
and you will never leave me to face my
    perils alone.

Thomas Merton

SOUL OF CHRIST

Soul of Christ, be my sanctification;
Body of Christ, be my salvation;
Blood of Christ, fill all my veins;
Water of Christ's side, wash out my stains;
Passion of Christ, my comfort be;
O good Jesus, listen to me:
In thy wounds I fain would hide,
Ne'er to be parted from thy side;
Guard me, should the foe assail me;
Call me when my life shall fail me;
Bid me come to thee above,
With thy saints to sing thy love
World without end. Amen.

Tr. John Henry Newman

TO CHRIST OUR ONLY TEACHER

Thank you, Jesus, for bringing me this far.
In your light I see the light of my life.
Your teaching is brief and to the point:
You persuade us to trust in our heavenly
    Father;
you command us to love one another.
What is easier than to believe in God?
What is sweeter than to love him?
Your yoke is pleasant, your burden is light,
you, the one and only Teacher!
You promise everything to those who obey
    your teaching;
you ask nothing too hard for a believer,
nothing a lover can refuse.
Your promises to your disciples are true,
entirely true, nothing but the truth.
Even more, you promise us yourself,
the perfection of all that can be made
    perfect.
Thank you, Jesus, now and always.
Amen.

Nicholas of Cusa

FOR GOD'S GOOD EARTH

Father,
the bible tells us
you looked on all that you made
and saw that it was good.
But we have been too willing
to squander the richness of creation.
We have laid the ax to the mighty forests
despoiled the green hillsides
wasted earth's mineral wealth.
We have fouled the air
littered the countryside
and polluted the streams and oceans.
Voices are raised
to stop us from squandering our patrimony.
May we heed them in time so that one day
we can look on the planet you have given
     us
and say with pride, once again,
"Behold, it is good."
Amen.

Christopher Prayer Book

FOR BROTHERHOOD

Father,
you have made us.
Red, yellow, brown, white and black
tall and short, fat and thin
rich and poor, young and old—
all are your children.
Teach us to cooperate rather than to
      compete
to respect rather than to revile
to forgive rather than condemn.
Your Son turned from no one.
May we learn, like him, to be open
to the share of the divine
that you have implanted
in each of your sons and daughters.
And may we forge a bond of love
that will make a living reality
the brotherhood in which we profess to
      believe.
Amen.

Christopher Prayer Book

FOR THE CHURCH

Gracious Father,
we pray to you for your holy Catholic
    Church.
Fill it with your truth.
Keep it in your peace.
Where it is corrupt, reform it.
Where it is in error, correct it.
Where it is right, defend it.
Where it is in want, provide for it.
Where it is divided, reunite it;
for the sake of your Son, our Savior Jesus
    Christ.
Amen.

William Laud

MY GIFT

Lord, I freely yield all my freedom to you.
Take my memory, my intellect and my
    entire will.
You have given me anything I am or have;
I give it all back to you to stand under your
    will alone.
Your love and your grace are enough for
    me;
I shall ask for nothing more.

St. Ignatius Loyola

TEACH ME TO STAND UP FREE

God, give me the courage to be
     revolutionary
As your Son Jesus Christ was.
Give me the courage to loosen myself
     from this world.
Teach me to stand up free
and to shun no criticism.
God, it is for your kingdom.
Make me free,
make me poor in this world.
Then will I be rich in the real world,
which this life is all about.
God, thank you for the vision of the future,
but make it fact and not just theory.

Henri Nouwen

FOR A LIGHT IN THE DARKNESS

Father, grant that I may be
a bearer of Christ Jesus, your Son.
Allow me to warm the often cold,
    impersonal
scene of modern life with your burning
    love.
Strengthen me, by your Holy Spirit
to carry out my mission of changing the
    world
or some definite part of it, for the better.
Despite my lamentable failures, bring home
    to me
that my advantages are your blessings
to be shared with others.
Make me more energetic in setting to rights
what I find wrong with the world
instead of complaining about it or myself.
Nourish in me a practical desire
to build up rather than tear down
to reconcile more than polarize
to go out on a limb rather than crave
    security.
Never let me forget that it is far better
to light one candle than to curse the
    darkness.
And to join my light, one day, with yours.
Amen.

Christopher Prayer Book

FOR A HOLY HEART

Lord, grant me a holy heart
    that sees always what is fine and pure
    and is not frightened at the sight of sin,
    but creates order wherever it goes.
Grant me a heart that knows nothing
    of boredom, weeping and sighing.
Let me not be too concerned
    with the bothersome thing
    I call "myself."
Lord, give me a sense of humor
    and I will find happiness in life
    and profit for others.

St. Thomas More

FOR COURAGE

Lord Jesus, teach me to be generous;
teach me to serve you as you deserve,
to give and not to count the cost,
to fight and not to heed the wounds,
to toil and not to seek for rest,
to labor and not to seek reward,
except that of knowing that I do your will.
Amen.

St. Ignatius Loyola

FOR JUSTICE AND PEACE

Almighty and eternal God,
may your grace enkindle in all of us
a love for the many unfortunate people
    whom poverty and misery reduce to a
      condition of life
    unworthy of human beings.
Arouse in the hearts of those who call you
    Father
a hunger and thirst for justice and peace,
    and for fraternal charity in deeds and in
      truth.
Grant, O Lord, peace in our days,
peace to souls, peace to families, peace to
    our country,
and peace among nations.
Amen.

Pope Pius XII

PRAYER TO MARY FOR THE SICK

Mary, health of the sick,
Be at the bedside of all the world's sick
       people;
  of those who are unconscious and
      dying;
  of those who have begun their agony;
  of those who have abandoned
  all hope of a cure;
  of those who weep and cry out in pain;
  of those who cannot receive care
  because they have no money;
  of those who ought to be resting
  but are forced by poverty to work;
  of those who seek vainly in their beds
  for a less painful position;
  of those who pass long nights
      sleepless;
  of those who are tormented
  by the cares of a family in distress;
  of those who must renounce
  their most cherished plans for the
      future;
  of those, above all,
  who do not believe in a better life;
  of those who rebel and curse God;
  of those who do not know that Christ
  suffered like them and for them.

Rabboni

FOR OUR COUNTRY

Lord Jesus, our brother and example,
immersed in history you were the subject
    of a mighty empire,
a lowly member of a conquered and
    occupied nation.
You understand the dangers of being a
    political being,
the challenge of serving God and Caesar
    both.
Help us to discover our higher loyalties
in the face of our lesser obligations.
Give us the insight and courage to criticize
    where necessary
and the grace to love and serve one another
    in the here and now.
Establish the reign of God in our hearts
and bring us to full citizenship in the
    kingdom of heaven,
where you live and reign for ever and
    ever.
Amen.

TRUTH AND BEAUTY

God our Father,
by the work of your Spirit, living in our
        hearts,
you lead men to desire your perfection,
to seek for truth and to rejoice for beauty.
Enlighten and inspire
all thinkers, writers, artists and craftsmen,
so that in all things which are true and
        pure and beautiful,
your name may be made holy
and your kingdom come on earth.
We ask this through Jesus Christ our
        Lord.

St. Anselm's Chapel, Canterbury Cathedral

FOR INSIGHT

May the Lord Jesus touch our eyes,
as he did those of the blind.
Then we shall begin to see
in visible things those which are invisible.
May he open our eyes to gaze,
not on present realities,
but on the blessings to come.
May he open the eyes of our heart
to contemplate God in Spirit,
through Jesus Christ the Lord, to whom
        belong
power and glory through all eternity.
Amen.

Origen

FOR LOVE AND SERVICE

Lord,
you created us for yourself
and our hearts are restless until they rest in
    you.
Please show us how to love you with all
    our hearts
and our neighbor as ourself.
Teach us to be practical about loving one
    another
in you and for you and as you desire.
Show us our immediate neighbor today;
the need of others is your call to our
    attention.
Remind us that you count as done to you
what we do for one another,
and that our turning away from one another
is really turning our backs on you.
Make us know, love and serve you in this
    life
and be happy for ever in the next
in union with all our sisters and brothers,
children of a common Father.
To serve you is to reign.
Amen.

FOR THOSE WE LOVE

Lord God,
we can hope for others nothing better
than the happiness we desire for ourselves.
Therefore, I pray you, do not separate me
    after death
from those I have tenderly loved on earth.
Grant that where I am they may be with me,
and that I may enjoy their presence in
    heaven
after being so often deprived of it on earth.
Lord God, I ask you to receive your beloved
    children
immediately into your life-giving heart.
After this brief life on earth,
give them eternal happiness.
Amen.

St. Ambrose of Milan

TO JOSEPH OUR PROTECTOR

Joseph, son of David,
do not be afraid to take Mary, your
wife,
into your own home.
She will give birth to a Son
and you shall call him Jesus,
for he shall save his people from their
sins.

Joseph did as the angel of the Lord
commanded him,
and received her into his home.

Father,
you entrusted our Savior to the care of
St. Joseph.
By the help of his prayers
may your Church continue to serve its
Lord, Jesus Christ,
who lives and reigns with you and the
Holy Spirit,
one God, for ever and ever.
Amen.

FOR SPIRITUAL GROWTH

Father,
you are able to accomplish immeasurably
     more
than we can ask or imagine.
Make us grasp fully, together with all the
     saints,
the breadth and the length, the height and
     the depth
of Christ's love, which surpasses all
     knowledge,
in order that we may be completely filled
with the utter fullness of God.

Father,
from whom every family in heaven and
     earth derives its origin,
grant us, out of your glorious riches,
to be strengthened through the Spirit
for the development of our inner selves,
and to have Christ dwelling through faith
     in our hearts
and to be rooted and grounded in love.
We ask this through the same Christ our
     Lord.
Amen.

Adapted from Ephesians 3

FOR THOSE WHO HAVE GONE
BEFORE US

The Lord will open to them the gates of
            paradise,
    and they will return to that homeland
    where there is no death, but only
            lasting joy.

Give them eternal rest, O Lord,
    and let them share your glory.

O God, our Creator and Redeemer,
    by your power Christ conquered death
    and returned to you in glory.
    May all your people who have gone
            before us in faith
    share his victory
    and enjoy the vision of your glory for
            ever,
    where Christ lives and reigns with you
            and the Holy Spirit,
    one God, for ever and ever.
Amen.

Roman Missal

WITH ALL MY HEART

My God, I desire to love you perfectly,
with all my heart, which you made for
    yourself,
with all my mind, which you alone can
    satisfy,
with all my soul, which longs to soar to you,
with all my strength, my feeble strength
which shrinks from so great a task
and yet can choose nothing else
but spend itself in loving you.
Claim my heart; free my mind;
uplift my soul; reinforce my strength;
that where I fail, you may succeed in me
and make me love you perfectly,
through Jesus Christ, my Lord.

Community of St. Mary the Virgin, Wantage

I AM READY . . . I ACCEPT

Father,
I abandon myself into your hands;
do with me what you will.
Whatever you may do, I thank you:
I am ready for all, I accept all.
Let only your will be done in me,
and in all your creatures—
I wish no more than this, O Lord.
Into your hands I commend my soul;
I offer it to you with all the love of my
     heart,
for I love you, Lord, and so need to give
     myself,
to surrender myself into your hands without
     reserve,
and with boundless confidence,
for you are my Father.

Charles de Foucauld

TO THE HOLY SPIRIT

Come, O Holy Spirit, come.
Come as the wind and cleanse;
come as the fire and burn;
convert and consecrate our lives
to our great good and your great glory;
through Jesus Christ our Lord.

FOR THE DYING

Lord,
this night some will be gathered to the
        Father.
Grant that they may go forth
surrounded by their loved ones,
without pain of body,
with clarity of mind,
and with joyful expectancy of soul.
Amen.

J. Massynberde Ford

II

Everyday Prayers

Some prayers are so familiar that they have a permanent place in our memory (Our Father, Hail Mary, etc.). Others, like Acts of Faith, Hope and Love, are familiar to us in one version or another.

Here, then, are some common prayers for quick reference if our memory falters.

THE LORD'S PRAYER

Our Father, who art in heaven,
hallowed be thy name;
thy kingdom come;
thy will be done on earth as it
    is in heaven.
Give us this day our daily bread;
and forgive us our trespasses
as we forgive those who trespass
    against us;
and lead us not into temptation,
but deliver us from evil.

For thine is the kingdom and the power and
    the glory for ever and ever. Amen.

THE HAIL MARY

Hail, Mary, full of grace, the Lord is with
    you.
Blessed are you among women,
and blessed is the fruit of your womb, Jesus.
Holy Mary, Mother of God, pray for us
    sinners,
        now and at the hour of our death.
Amen.

THE DOXOLOGY

Glory to the Father, and to the Son, and
to the Holy Spirit:
as it was in the beginning, is now, and
will be for ever. Amen.

THE APOSTLES' CREED

I believe in God, the Father almighty,
creator of heaven and earth.

I believe in Jesus Christ, his only Son, our
Lord.
He was conceived by the power of the
Holy Spirit
and born of the Virgin Mary.
He suffered under Pontius Pilate,
was crucified, died, and was
buried.
He descended to the dead.
On the third day he rose again.
He ascended into heaven,
and is seated at the right hand of
the Father.
He will come again to judge the living
and the dead.

I believe in the Holy Spirit,
    the holy catholic Church,
    the communion of saints,
    the forgiveness of sins,
    the resurrection of the body,
    and the life everlasting.

COME HOLY SPIRIT

Come, Holy Spirit, fill the hearts of your
    faithful
    and kindle in them the fire of your love.

Send forth your Spirit, and they shall be
    created:
    And you will renew the face of the
      earth.

O God,
on the first Pentecost you instructed the
    hearts of those who believed in you
by the light of the Holy Spirit:
under the inspiration of the same Spirit,
give us a taste for what is right and true
and a continuing sense of his joy-bringing
    presence and power:
through Jesus Christ our Lord.
Amen.

GRACE BEFORE MEALS

All living things look to you
    to give them their food in due season.
You give it, they gather it up:
    you open your hand, they have their fill.
Glory to the Father, and to the Son, and to
        the Holy Spirit:
    as it was in the beginning, is now, and
        will be for ever. Amen.

Bless us, O Lord, and these your gifts
which we are about to receive from your
    bounty,
through Christ our Lord.
Amen.

GRACE AFTER MEALS

Let all the works of the Lord bless the Lord,
    and his children shall praise him for
        ever.
Glory to the Father, and to the Son, and to
        the Holy Spirit:
    as it was in the beginning, is now, and
        will be for ever. Amen.

We give you thanks, Almighty God,
for these and all your blessings;
you live and reign for ever and ever.
Amen.

AN ACT OF FAITH

O God,
I firmly believe all the truths that you have
     revealed
and that you teach us through your Church,
for you are truth itself
and can neither deceive nor be deceived.

AN ACT OF HOPE

O God,
I hope with complete trust that you will
     give me,
through the merits of Jesus Christ,
all necessary grace in this world
and everlasting life in the world to come,
for this is what you have promised
and you always keep your promises.

AN ACT OF CHARITY

O God,
I love you with my whole heart above all
     things,
because you are infinitely good;
and for your sake I love my neighbor as I
     love myself.

AN ACT OF CONTRITION

O God,
I am sorry with my whole heart for all my
    sins
because you are Goodness itself
and sin is an offense against you.
Therefore I firmly resolve,
with the help of your grace,
not to sin again and to avoid the occasions
    of sin.

HAIL HOLY QUEEN

Hail, holy Queen, mother of mercy,
our life, our sweetness, and our hope.
To you do we cry,
poor banished children of Eve.
To you do we send up our sighs,
mourning and weeping in this vale of tears.
Turn then, most gracious advocate,
your eyes of mercy toward us,
and after this exile
show to us the blessed fruit of your
    womb, Jesus.
O clement, O loving,
O sweet Virgin Mary.

THE ANGELUS

The angel of the Lord brought the message
      to Mary.
       And she conceived of the Holy Spirit.
         Hail Mary . . .

I am the Lord's servant;
      May it happen to me as you have said.
        Hail Mary . . .

And the Word was made flesh;
      And dwelt among us.
        Hail Mary . . .

Pray for us, O holy Mother of God;
      that we may be made worthy of the
        promises of Christ.

Pour forth, O Lord,
your grace into our hearts,
that we to whom the incarnation of Christ
      your son
was made known by the message of an
      angel,
may by his passion and cross be brought to
      the glory of his resurrection;
through the same Christ our Lord.
Amen.

THE MEMORARE

Remember, O most gracious Virgin Mary,
that never was it known that anyone who
    fled to your protection,
implored your help, or sought your inter-
    cession was left unaided.
Inspired by this confidence, we fly unto
    you,
O Virgin of virgins, our Mother!
To you we come, before you we stand,
    sinful and sorrowful.
O Mother of the Word incarnate,
despise not our petitions,
but in your mercy hear and answer us.
Amen.

QUEEN OF HEAVEN

Joy fill your heart, O Queen most high,
    alleluia!
Your Son who in the tomb did lie, alleluia!
Has risen as he did prophesy, alleluia!
Pray for us, Mother, when we die, alleluia!

III

Student Life

Students have special needs and concerns, like examinations and ill-tempered teachers. Here are prayers which touch that experience in some way.

By reading these prayers and reflecting on them, you may better understand where your life is going. Or at least you will find that others share your confusion!

Some prayers in this section were written by students, others by teachers, and at least one — the first — was written by a saint.

BEFORE STUDY

Creator of all things,
true source of light and wisdom, lofty
    origin of all being,
graciously let a ray of your brilliance
penetrate into the darkness of my under-
    standing
and take from me the double darkness in
    which I have been born,
an obscurity of both sin and ignorance.
Give me a sharp sense of understanding,
a retentive memory,
and the ability to grasp things correctly and
    fundamentally.
Grant me the talent of being exact in my
    explanations,
and the ability to express myself with
    thoroughness and charm.
Point out the beginning, direct the progress,
and help in the completion;
through Christ our Lord.
Amen.

St. Thomas Aquinas

OPEN MY MIND

Lord Jesus,
you were once a student like me.
You studied God's law, the history of your
    people
and a trade by which to earn a living.
You lived in a human family,
made steady progress in understanding
and yearned to discover your vocation in
    life.
Open my mind to the truth of things,
make me humble before the awesome
    mysteries of the universe,
make me proud to be a human being and
    a child of God
and give me courage to live my life in the
    light of your gospel.
Amen.

THE BALANCE

Help me, God, to find a balance
between study and leisure.
When work must be done,
let me realize that I am here to learn
and cannot go to every party.

Let me also see that
life is more than books
and being a person comes before grades.

A snowball battle,
a walk around a lake
or a simple talk with a friend
will do wonders
when studies get me down.
Guide me along this balanced line.
Amen.

Loretta Mirandola

ANYTHING CAN BE ACCOMPLISHED

It's never easy to be a student.
Every day brings more assignments until
    it seems
that the hard work will never end.

I know I'd rather watch TV or listen to
    records
many times when I sit down to study,
but please, Lord, help me to realize
that knowledge, like your love, can never
    be lost.

Help me never to underestimate myself as
    a student
because anything can be accomplished
with your guidance and love.
Let me be helpful and understanding
toward my fellow students,
and not judge them but radiate the same
    love
you show us through your lasting mercy.
Amen.

Bill Starr

PRAYER FOR INSIGHT

Lord, I can't even imagine
why you have given me this roommate,
these teachers and books,
the problem at home,
a good friend who seems remote and distant
at times.

I wonder about my dark side too—
the way my flesh takes over, my
       unbelievable selfishness
and desire to dominate a conversation
or a friendship.

And, yes, I worry because you seem
so distant and remote from me, too,
and have so little part to play in my life.

I don't really expect you to give me
all the answers on a computer printout.
But I ask for a little more insight into
       myself and others,
and a little more understanding about the
       things
which crowd my day.
And when it is dark help me realize
that you are with me in the darkness.
Amen.

FOR A PRE-MED

Father,
I have chosen a profession of compassion.
> Help me to be kind to my fellow
> students.
I have feelings of rivalry.
> Help me to be a friend.
I have many hours of doubt.
> Help me to be sure.
I have a long and strenuous path.
> Help me to endure it.
I see much wrong with medicine today.
> Help me to correct it.
I have felt the helplessness of the sick and
> dying.
> Help me to heal and comfort them.

And most of all help me
> "To work as if everything depended
> on me,
> To pray as if everything depended on
> you."
Amen.

Kevin C. Kelleher

JESUS IN EVERYDAY LIFE

I see you Jesus
no longer just in my prayer,
no longer just in my bible,
but in the breaking of the bread of
      everyday life.
I see you Jesus
when you help me get done what's got to
      get done:
my homework, my finals, my everyday
      living.
Where do I see you?
More and more in the people around me:
my friends, the people at the dinner table,
my Mom and Dad, my sister, the guy on the
      bus home.
You have become flesh in them;
you are not just the Spirit in the sky any
      longer,
but you are right here in them to love me,
      for me to love.
How right it is to know that I can love them,
and in loving them love you yourself.
I feel so much more a part of them, a part of
      you,
and that's all I ever really wanted anyway.

Thanks for entering everyday life.
I'm glad I don't have to go to the desert to
    find you.
All I have to do is listen right here and now
and I'll find you coming through,
gently, subtly touching my heart with your
    love and wisdom.
I'm happy you love me just the way I am,
helping me develop all the potential that's
    in me,
all the potential that's in the world,
your precious gifts of every day.
Amen.

Dan McGraw

PRAYER BEFORE EXAMINATIONS

Lord,
it seems as though our lives
are one test after another,
weighing us in somebody's balance.

Save us from taking the coming tests
too seriously or too lightly,
but grant that we may reflect
the best of the work we've done
and the best of the teaching we've received;
through Jesus Christ our Lord.
Amen.

John W. Vannorsdall

FOR RESPONSIBLE DECISIONS

O God,
who has called me to place such complete
    trust in you
that nothing can tyrannize my life,
deliver me, I pray . . .

    from becoming a slave to my books
    from daydreaming away my time
    from an overconcern about sex
    from an overanxiety about my future
    from an uncritical view of myself
    from an overcritical view of myself

and from all the half-known deities
which try to dictate what I shall be.
Save me, that I may be free
to make responsible decisions
and serve you with wholeness.
Amen.

John W. Vannorsdall

A NURSE'S PRAYER

Christ,
may we who are preparing to be nurses
work with devotion.
May we touch with gentleness;
may we speak with tenderness;
may we listen with our eyes
as well as our ears.
May we smile from the heart;
may we understand with deep feeling;
may we know the time to be quiet . . .
    the time to laugh,
    the time to sympathize,
    the time to encourage.
And above all,
may we know
that the time to love
is now!
Lord,
hear our prayer.
Amen.

Adapted from a prayer by Marjorie Gray

CADET PRAYER

Heavenly King,
Yours is the only true sovereignty;
Yours is the world and all that is in it.

Yet you have given to men stewardship
    over your realm.
Grant us, therefore, your wisdom in the
    discharge of our duties;
Guide our leaders in the way of peace;
And show each of us your will.

Help us to care for our subordinates,
    to have patience with them,
    to give due respect to our leaders.
Teach us to pray for our enemies,
    to love those who hate us,
    to show mercy to our prisoners.

But above all grant to us discernment of
    true justice and the courage to seek it,
So that when you come again in glory, you
    may receive a world holy and pleasing
    in your sight.

James M. Backes

A FASTING PRAYER

Father, I'm hungry.
The day has been a long one,
and it's far from being over.
The thought of food keeps coming to mind,
and I've even debated breaking this fast
because it hurts so much to be hungry.
But, more than that, it's the whole feeling
    of weakness
and even a little unavoidable sadness
that comes with an empty stomach.
I'm not asking you to take away the pain,
    Lord,
but just give me the strength to endure it
    with heart,
because I keep thinking about my brothers
    and sisters,
some of them little children
who have nothing to eat tonight
and may die tomorrow.
Show them your mercy, Father,
and please forgive me.
Amen.

Paul Beaudette

MY FUTURE

Jesus, my Lord, my friend—
Tonight my brother called
to tell me I am an aunt!
Thank you, thank you for
a new life in a new baby boy.
I think of them and wonder . . .
Will I someday be a mother too?

But right now
there are thoughts of
my life turning
on a path that would
be service to you in
the Church.
I can see myself—
teaching children,
helping to minister
      to all kinds of persons
along with others
who have chosen to do the same.

What is right for me?
What do you see in my future?
It would be easier if
I could see as you do—clearly.
But things are not clear now.

I only know that I have some feelings.
Give me vision,
help me to live well now.
Give me courage
and friends who support me.
Amen.

WHILE OTHERS SUFFER

There's a lot of suffering in the world.
Lord, you know that better than I do.
Poverty, sickness, and hunger;
        pain, loneliness, and fear.
You never promised us paradise in this
        world
but I can't help feeling guilty for having
        so much
when so many have so little.
I know their suffering is partly my fault,
because, even while I don't actively will it,
I know that I affirm it by living the com-
        fortable kind of life I do.
Please forgive me, Father,
        but more than that,
instill in me an active, genuine awareness
        and concern

for those whose suffering I don't really
   know,
so that I might find a life-style more in line
   with their suffering,
and do what little I can to help their
   situation.
For there are basic things
that should be theirs regardless,
because they are my brothers and sisters
and your sons and daughters.
Amen.

Paul Beaudette

FOR FRIENDS

Help me to be a friend to all who need me.
Show me how to share your love,
teach me to see you in others.
While I'm here in school,
let me see that more important
than any books or exams
are the friends I make,
the friends I'll come to love and cherish
and always remember.
Amen.

Joe Corpora

FOR HOME

Thank you, Lord, for my home—
    memories of younger years
    and the loving warmth
    which never fails to greet
    the prodigal steps of my college years.
For the timeless sense of belonging I find
        there,
    I give quiet thanks,
    knowing that whenever you are
        present—
    I am home.
    Amen.

Anne Kaiser

THE CAFETERIA

Today I complained about the food in the
    cafeteria.
Forgive me, Lord.
Instead of complaining let me be thankful
    for the food I ate.
There are so many who will die of hunger
    today in this world.
I feel ashamed of having complained.
    Forgive me.
Amen.

Joe Corpora

THE PARTY

Lord, I really had a good time
    at the party last night.
It wasn't one of those big parties
    where there is a lot of noise and
        confusion.

In fact, there were only a few of us
    and we were fairly quiet (though a
    neighbor poked his head in once and
    asked us to keep it down).

We shared some laughs and talked about
    some deep things, too.
Because of the party, I know some people
    better now,
    and like them more.
They are my friends now, more than ever.
    Thank you.
Amen.

CHAMPION

I'm a good basketball player and a poor
    musician;
I've finally realized I'm not a superman
    at everything I do.
And even though Wheaties are the
    Breakfast of Champions,
Their whole wheat flakes will not make
    me the kind of champion you want.
Jesus, help me to live with enthusiasm;
    to see a listless stranger and to talk to
        him;
    to give a word of encouragement to a
        floundering student;
    to be patient with my roommate even
        when he is wrong;
    to donate to charity even though
        world hunger will still exist;
    to accept you as my savior and
    to trust you as my friend.
Amen.

Jim Kelleher

FOR GOOD ATTITUDES TOWARD SEX

Sometimes I feel like I am going crazy.
I've got all this sex-drive going in me,
pounding in me, burning in me, tantalizing
    me.
It delights and yet disturbs me;
it confuses and bewilders me.
What I do about it often bothers me
and makes me feel rotten about myself.
How should I think about sex, Lord?
How should I express my growing sexuality?
What is the real truth about sex and sexual
    love?

In the Creed we say you are the Creator
    of heaven and earth
and that your Son actually took flesh for
    our sake;
you must know more about sex than we do!
Sex must be a part of your lovely plan for us,
and since your Son became a sexual being
    like us
the truth about sex must come from
a deeper, fuller understanding of the
    Word-made-flesh
who came and dwelt among us.

In my confusion make me realize, first of all,
that sex is one of your finest gifts.

Being afraid of it or being ashamed of it
is no way to thank you for it!
Because my sexuality is your personal gift
    to me,
help me to accept it graciously
and to use it thankfully,
with full human responsibility.
And that is asking a lot!
Amen.

EARNEST DESIRE

Lord God, when you made me in my
    mother's womb,
you fashioned me as a man,
with all the longings and desires that are a
    man's.
As I grow now into the possession of my
    manhood,
of my powers of affection and of under-
    standing,
I wish to offer them back to you
as an appropriate sacrifice of praise and
    thanksgiving.
You have created me to share life with one
    particular woman,
for though there are many I could marry,
there is one alone to whom I shall pledge
    my life.

For her I long, confident that we shall
    meet in your good time.

Our young bodies will find fulfillment in
    each other,
our souls will progress together toward
    union with you.

I anticipate her, then, and the mutual gift,
    yours and ours.
I am young enough to be utterly
    enthusiastic,
old enough to be discerning,
and experienced enough to rely upon you
    and to seek your will alone.
Let us get on with it, then, with humility
    and earnest desire.

James M. Schellman

FOR A PARTNER IN MARRIAGE

Heavenly Father,
from the very beginning you wanted men
    and women to find love
and create new life in marriage.
Marriage is a mystery of your love for us
and of our faithful love for each other.
Help us prepare seriously for a marriage in
    Christ
who calls us to a union of true affection
and strengthens our resolves in the
    sacrament of Matrimony.
Give us sensitive hearts, discerning minds
    and ready wills,

eager to serve you and to discover the truth
     of each other.
Nourish our bourgeoning sexuality
and direct it to good and honest ends.
On our wedding day unite us before your
     altar,
feed us with the body and blood of your
     Christ
and become the common center of our
     hearts and of our home.
Amen.

PRAYER FOR THE RIGHT CHOICE

I just found out, Lord,
that the couple next door at home
are getting divorced.

It really threw me into shock—they always
     seemed
as happy as any other middle-aged couple
     I know.
I wonder about the tension and strain and
     unhappiness
that must have been there all those years
when they smiled and waved
and invited us over in the summer for a
     barbecue.

Lord, I feel sorry for them and for their
     children.
Help them all to find their way.

But what I'm also feeling, Lord,
is that no marriage is a sure thing—
including the one I'll be part of sooner or
    later.

I ask you, Lord, to help me find the right
    man
(though you know I'm no prize myself!).
May he be strong when I am weak,
brave when I am afraid,
and willing to share his strength with me
as I am willing to share mine with him.

Finally, I ask that you be present to both of
    us in our life together.
Amen.

FOR MY FIANCEE

Lord,
she and I have set the date.
I've never known anything so sure in all
    my life.
Lord, I love her.
It's just so right.
So right, too, to thank you.
To thank you for what you've given me as
        a person:
    my talents, my abilities, my self.

I thank you for my family,
    my brothers and sisters.
In a unique way they all have something
    to do with this.
Thanks for her, and her family,
    and all that made her.
The experts have little to say to me,
now that I've experienced love.
And you, Lord, you are what we share.
I love you, too.
Bless our marriage. Draw us to you.
We're a trinity: she and you and I.
Amen.

FOR CHOOSING A CALLING

Dear Father,
you are the creative origin of all I am
and of all I am called to be.
With the talents and opportunities I have,
how may I serve you best?
Please guide my mind and heart,
open me to the needs of my country and
    of the world,
and help me to choose wisely and
    practically
for your honor and glory
and for the good of all those whose lives
    I touch.
Amen.

CLEAR AWAY THE COBWEBS

Sometimes, Lord,
I think that I will go through life
always switching my major at the last
     minute.
When I am really honest with myself
I realize that I simply don't know
what I want to do after I leave here.

I've gone through the astronaut stage,
and played out the football fantasy
to the last winning touchdown.
Now it's time to start making plays
     in the real world,
and my head is not screwed on straight.

You needn't send a special-delivery letter
but it would be helpful, Lord,
if you would clear away a few of the
     cobwebs
and help me decide what you want me to
     do
with the raw material I have received.
Amen.

PRAYER OF A SEMINARIAN

Lord,
I want to serve you as your priest.
I may not have very much,
but what I have I give you—
health, a few brains, a talent or two,
and a sincere desire to do what you want.

Lord, teach me to mold that desire into
     action,
to channel my selfishness into service of
     others.
Help me to bring companionship to the
     lonely,
          comfort to the oppressed,
          direction to the lost.
Grant that I may one day be the kind of
     priest
you want me to be.
Amen.

Donald Franks

I PLACE THEM IN YOUR CARE

Lord Jesus Christ,
I praise and thank you for my parents and
    my brothers and sisters
whom you have given me to cherish.
Surround them with your tender, loving
    care,
teach them to love and serve one another in
    true affection
and to look to you in all their needs
I place them all in your care,
knowing that your love for them is
    greater than my own.
Keep us close to one another in this life
and conduct us at the last to our true and
    heavenly home.
Blessed be God for ever.
Amen.

FOR ATHLETES

Thanks, Lord, for giving me life; and talents
    for my participation in sports.

Help me to play well, to use my powers to
    the full, to see them as gifts from you.

Be with me when I need to play hurt, when
    I have to deal with the pain of injury,
    disappointment, loss.

Keep me aware of the brotherhood I have
    with all men, even when they are op-
    ponents; free me from the temptation
    to fake, to foul, to cheat.

I need to see that dedication to the cause
    will mean suffering, but let me know
    that it is a kind of suffering that leads to
    new life and greater maturity.

Help me play with heart, and never lose
    heart.

Most of all, help me never to quit in my
    efforts to be open to you. For I
    believe your full coming into my life is
    the way to real life, in all I do; I believe
    it is the way of my becoming the truly
    human person you destined me to be.

Amen.

FOR MY FAMILY

I want to pray for my family.
So what do I say?
I've got so many mixed feelings, Lord.
I love them, I really do.
And another whole part of me says—
I'm different.
The blood that runs through us,
my brothers and sisters, my mother and
     father
binds us. We are one,
but not one.

I'll make my own family someday soon,
and my loyalties will go with them.
But for now I realize as never before
how much my family is a part of me.
Bless them, be good to them,
let them know I love them
now that I've "grown up."
Amen.

FOR PARENTS IN TROUBLE

Lord, you are present everywhere.
We ask your help for those of our parents
who are in trouble.
Where they are at odds with each other,
we pray for a breakthrough and reconcilia-
    tion.
Where a job has been lost,
grant a new opportunity for useful work.
Where there is sickness,
we pray for healing and strength.
Where there are patterns which make life
    dull,
we pray for a broken routine
which will allow new possibilities.
O Lord,
some of our parents have trouble.
We ask you to help them,
and to help us to know what to do;
through Jesus Christ our Lord.
Amen.

John W. Vannorsdall

MORNING PRAYER TO THE HOLY SPIRIT

O Holy and astounding Spirit,
You catch me by surprise at least once a day
    with the freshness of your love
    and the unpredictability of your
        presence—
    especially in humble things
    that somehow give me immense joy.
Some moments are completely new, full of
        joy,
    as uplifting as the dawning sun,
    and those moments come from you,
        day by day.
Stand behind me today when I'm right and
    ought to be more determined,
    and block my way when I'm being
        stupid and ought to back off.
Teach me true compassion for those in
    need,
    so I can be of genuine help to someone.
Bless me, today, Holy Spirit, and astound me
    again!

Tom Noe

A NIGHT PRAYER

O God, before I sleep,
I remember before you all the people I love,
and now in the silence I say their names to
you.
All the people who are sad and lonely, old
and forgotten,
poor and hungry and cold,
in pain of body and in distress of mind.
Bless all who specially need your blessing,
and bless me too,
and make this a good night for me.
This I ask for your love's sake.
Amen.

William Barclay

THE PATH

When my mind is dark
and my thoughts empty.
When the images are frozen
and my mind meaningless.

Help me to recognize
that your love is with me.
Guide me to the path
where my love will flow again.
Amen.

David Kollar

IV

A Sampling of Psalms

Century after century the Book of Psalms has contributed more to Jewish and Christian Prayer than any other book of the bible. These ancient hymns and poetic compositions seem to speak to the needs of believers in every generation. In supplying simple, noble texts they become a school of prayer, teaching us little by little how we should address our Father in heaven. They were Jesus' own school of prayer and we can hardly do better than follow in his footsteps. In addition to the psalms contained in the morning and evening prayer section (pp. 155-202), the following favorite psalms will appeal to many and will apply to a variety of situations, moods and needs.

Psalm 8

GOD'S GLORY AND MAN'S DIGNITY

Lord, our Lord,
  your greatness is seen in all the
    world!
Your praise reaches up to the heavens;
  it is sung by children and babies.
You have built a fortress against your foes
  to stop your enemies and adversaries.

When I look at the sky, which you have
    made,
  at the moon and the stars, which you set
    in their places—
what is man, that you think of him;
  mere man, that you care for him?

Yet you made him inferior only to your-
    self;
  you crowned him with glory and honor.
You made him ruler over all you have
    made;
  you placed him over all things:
sheep and cattle, and wild animals too;
  the birds and the fish,
    and all the creatures in the seas.

Lord, our Lord,
  your greatness is seen in all the world!

Psalm 19

THE HANDWRITING IN THE HEAVENS

How clearly the sky reveals God's glory!
   How plainly it shows what he has done!
Each day announces it to the following day;
   each night repeats it to the next.
No speech or words are used,
   no sound is heard;
yet their voice goes out to all the world,
   their message reaches the ends of the
      earth.

God set up a tent in the sky for the sun;
   it comes out like a bridegroom striding
      from his house,
   like an athlete, eager to run a race.
It starts at one end of the sky
   and goes around to the other.
   Nothing can hide from its heat.

Psalm 22 A CRY OF ANGUISH

My God, my God, why have you
   abandoned me?
I have cried desperately for help,
   but it still does not come!
During the day I call to you, my God,
   but you do not answer;
I call at night,
   but get no rest.
But you are enthroned as the Holy One,
   the one whom Israel praises.

Our ancestors put their trust in you;
   they trusted you, and you saved them.
They called to you and escaped from dan-
      ger;
   they trusted in you and were not disap-
      pointed.

But I am no longer a man; I am a worm,
   despised and scorned by all!
All who see me make fun of me;
   they stick out their tongues and shake
      their heads.
"You relied on the Lord," they say. "Why
      doesn't he save you?
   If the Lord likes you, why doesn't he
      help you?"

It was you who brought me safely through
    birth,
    and when I was a baby you kept me safe.
I have relied on you since I was born;
    since my birth you have been my God.
Do not stay away from me!
    Trouble is near,
    and there is no one to help.
Many enemies surround me like bulls;
    they are all around me,
    like fierce bulls from the land of Bashan.
They open their mouths like lions,
    roaring and tearing at me.

My strength is gone,
    gone like water spilled on the ground.
All my bones are out of joint;
    my heart feels like melted wax inside me.
My throat is as dry as dust,
    and my tongue sticks to the roof of my
        mouth.
You have left me for dead in the dust.

A gang of evil men is around me;
    like a pack of dogs, they close in on me;
    they tear my hands and feet.
All my bones can be seen.
My enemies look at me and stare;

they divide my clothes among themselves
and gamble for my robe.
Don't stay away from me, Lord!
Hurry and help me, my Savior!
Save me from the sword;
save my life from those dogs.
Rescue me from those lions;
I am helpless before those wild bulls.

Psalm 23 THE LORD IS MY SHEPHERD

The Lord is my shepherd;
  I have everything I need.
He lets me rest in fields of green grass
    and leads me to quiet pools of fresh
      water.
      He gives me new strength.

He guides me in the right way,
  as he has promised.
Even if that way goes through deepest
    darkness,
  I will not be afraid, Lord,
  because you are with me!
Your shepherd's rod and staff keep me safe.

You prepare a banquet for me,
  where all my enemies can see me;
you welcome me by pouring ointment on
    my head
  and filling my cup to the brim.
Certainly your goodness and love will be
    with me as long as I live;
  and your house will be my home forever.

Psalm 51 AN ACT OF CONTRITION

Be merciful to me, God,
    because of your constant love;
wipe away my sins,
    because of your great mercy!
Wash away my evil,
    and make me clean from my sin!

I recognize my faults;
    I am always conscious of my sins.
I have sinned against you—only against
        you,
    and done what you consider evil.
So you are right in judging me;
    you are justified in condemning me.
I have been evil from the time I was born;
    from the day of my birth I have been
        sinful.

A faithful heart is what you want;
    fill my mind with your wisdom.
Remove my sin, and I will be clean;
    wash me, and I will be whiter than snow.
Let me hear the sounds of joy and gladness;
    and though you have crushed and
        broken me,

I will be happy once again.
Close your eyes to my sins,
   and wipe out all my evil.

Create a pure heart in me, God,
   and put a new and loyal spirit in me.
Do not banish me from your presence;
   do not take your Holy Spirit away from
      me.
Give me again the joy that comes from your
      salvation,
   and make my spirit obedient.
Then I will teach sinners your commands,
   and they will turn back to you.

Spare my life, God my Savior,
   and I will gladly proclaim your right-
      eousness.
Help me to speak, Lord,
   and I will praise you.

Psalm 100 A HYMN OF PRAISE

Sing for joy to the Lord, all the world!
  Worship the Lord gladly,
  and come before him with joyful songs!

Never forget that the Lord is God!
  He made us, and we belong to him;
  we are his people, we are his flock.

Enter his temple with thanksgiving,
  go into his sanctuary with praise!
  Give thanks to him and praise him!

The Lord is good;
  his love lasts forever,
  and his faithfulness for all time.

Psalm 127
UNLESS THE LORD BUILD THE HOUSE

If the Lord does not build the house,
    the work of the builders is useless;
if the Lord does not protect the city,
    it does no good for the sentries to stand
        guard.
It is useless to work so hard for a living,
    getting up early and going to bed late,
    because the Lord gives rest to those he
        loves.

Children are a gift from the Lord;
    they are a real blessing.
The sons a man has when he is young
    are like arrows in a soldier's hand.
Happy is the man who has many such
        arrows!
He will never be defeated
    when he meets his enemies in the place
        of judgment.

Psalm 139 THE HOUND OF HEAVEN

Lord, you have examined me, and you
 know me.
You know everything I do;
 from far away you understand all my
 thoughts.
You see me, whether I am working or
 resting;
 you know all my actions.
Even before I speak
 you already know what I will say.
You are all around me, on every side;
 you protect me with your power.
Your knowledge of me is overwhelming;
 it is too deep for me to understand.

Where could I go to escape from your
 spirit?
 Where could I get away from your presence?
If I went up to heaven, you would be there;
 if I lay down in the world of the dead,
 you would be there.
If I flew away beyond the east,
 or lived in the farthest place in the west,
you would be there to lead me,
 you would be there to help me.
I could ask the darkness to hide me,
 or the light around me to turn into night,

but even the darkness is not dark for you,
and the night is as bright as the day.
Darkness and light are the same to you.

You created every part of me;
you put me together in my mother's
womb.
I praise you because you are to be feared;
all you do is strange and wonderful.
I know it with all my heart.
You saw my bones being formed,
carefully put together in my mother's
womb,
when I was growing there in secret.
You saw me before I was born.
The days that have been created for me
had all been recorded in your book,
before any of them had ever begun.
God, how difficult your thoughts are for me;
how many of them there are!
If I counted them, they would be more
than the grains of sand.
When I awake, I am still with you.

Examine me, God, and know my mind;
test me, and discover my thoughts.
Find out if there is any deceit in me,
and guide me in the eternal way.

Psalm 145

GOD'S GRANDEUR AND GOODNESS

I will proclaim your greatness, my God
    and king;
  I will thank you forever and ever.
Every day I will thank you;
  I will praise you forever and ever.
The Lord is great, and must be highly
    praised;
    his greatness is beyond understanding.

What you have done will be praised from
    one generation to the next;
  they will proclaim your mighty acts.
Men will speak of your glory and majesty,
  and I will meditate on your wonderful
    deeds.

Men will speak of your mighty acts,
  and I will proclaim your greatness.
They will tell about all your goodness,
  and sing about your kindness.

The Lord is loving and merciful,
    slow to become angry and full of constant
    love.
He is good to everyone
  and has compassion on all he made.

All your creatures, Lord, will praise you,
  and your people will give you thanks!
They will speak of the glory of your kingdom,
  and tell of your might,
so that all men will know your mighty acts,
  and the glorious majesty of your kingdom.
Your kingdom is eternal,
  and you are king forever.

The Lord is faithful to his promises,
  and good in all he does.
He helps all who are in trouble;
  he raises all who are humbled.
All living things look hopefully to him,
  and he gives them food when they need it.
He gives them enough
  and satisfies the needs of all.
The Lord is righteous in all he does,
  merciful in all his acts.
He is near to all who call to him,
  who call to him with sincerity.
He supplies the needs of all who fear him;
  he hears their cry and saves them.
He protects all who love him,
  but he will destroy all the wicked.
I will always praise the Lord;
  let all creatures praise his holy name forever!

Psalm 148 PRAISE THE LORD!

Praise the Lord!
Praise the Lord from heaven,
   you that live in the heights above!
Praise him, all his angels,
   all his heavenly armies!

Praise him, sun and moon;
   praise him, shining stars!
Praise him, highest heavens,
   and the waters above the sky!

Let them all praise the name of the Lord!
He commanded, and they were created;
   by his command they were fixed in their
      places forever,
   and they cannot disobey.

Praise the Lord from the earth,
   sea monsters and all ocean depths;
lightning and hail, snow and clouds,
   strong winds that obey his command!

Praise him, hills and mountains,
   fruit trees and forests;

all animals, tame and wild,
   reptiles and birds!

Praise him, kings and all peoples,
   princes and all other rulers;
young men and girls,
   old people and children also!

Let them all praise the name of the Lord.
His name is greater than all others;
   his glory is above earth and heaven!
He made his nation strong,
   so that all his people praise him,
   the people of Israel, so dear to him!

Praise the Lord!

God has filled the world with his likeness.
                        Paul Claudel

V

Quiet Time

Despite his incredibly busy public life, Jesus found time for prayerful reflection in solitude (Lk 5:15-16). Eastern mysticism and the entire Christian tradition tell us we must do the same.

Scripture offers a limitless resource of material for meditation. We can read favorite passages over and over again and still gain insight. For example, the Sermon on the Mount (Mt 5, 6, 7); the True Relations of Jesus (Mt 12:46-50); and the Parables of the Kingdom (Mt 13).

Others meditate by saying very slowly classic prayers such as the Lord's Prayer, the Creed, a favorite psalm, or by means of such devotions as the Rosary or the Way of the Cross. Still others will find material for reflection in some prayers in this book which are less well known but have power nonetheless.

Additionally, here are five examples of meditation, a traditional style of prayer which has appealed to many Christians in recent years:

1) A New Testament meditation on Christ,
2) a meditation on a verse of scripture,
3) a meditation on something ordinary,
4) an introspective meditation,
5) a paraphrase of a psalm.

1. JESUS CHRIST IS THE LORD

He always had the very nature of God
But he did not think that by force he should
    try to become equal with God.
Instead, of his own free will he gave it all up,
And took the nature of a servant.
He became like a man, he appeared in
    human likeness;
He was humble and walked the path of
    obedience to death—his death on the
    cross.
For this reason God raised him to the
    highest place above,
And gave him the name that is greater than
    any other name,
So that, in honor of the name of Jesus,
All beings in heaven, and on the earth, and
    in the world below
Will fall on their knees,
And all will openly proclaim that Jesus
    Christ is the Lord,
To the glory of God the Father.—Phil 2:6-11

2. TEACH US TO PRAY

"We do not know how to pray as we ought . . ."

Romans 8:26

The early ones of us, O Lord,
asked you how to pray.
You answered only with your life
saying nothing about the what
or how of effective words.
You conducted no workshops,
gave no formulas,
but only one sign,
the sign of Jonas and others
who came to terms with God
and lived through it barely.
Jonas prayed while running
away from the burning
call of you.
The prayer of Jacob was
a divine wrestling all night,
a going on with blessing in
his ears, limping in his legs.
Tortured Job's prayer was
of manure, flies, cruel fate
and the theology chatter
of his preacher friends.
Prayer for Moses was the struggle
that ripped him away

from the shepherd peace
he wanted so desperately.
Jeremiah sought only a
middle-class life, a wife,
some ground to call his own.
Prayer for him was cursing
out God from jail.
Habakkuk prayed by asking
why believe in one whose
holy promise history mocks.
Paul had it out with God
over the thorn in his flesh
and all he ever got was "no."
We would learn to pray, O Lord,
yet we shrink from true
coming to terms with you.
Help us to and through
Gethsemane, be with
our wrestling, our grappling
with destiny and you.
You know well what a
horrid place is prayer.
Coax us into this holy line
of battered men who
got through to you
and found themselves.

James Carroll

3. PRAYER ON A PENCIL

I was just sitting here, Lord,
doodling with my pencil,
when it struck me as something strange.
Here was a sharpened lead pencil,
common to me since kindergarten,
yet odd at the same time.
It was graphite from Pennsylvania,
timber from Oregon,
rubber from Brazil,
all stamped together in one instrument
intended for my personal use.
It was all those people
in all those places—
down in coal mines,
high up in mountains,
deep in steaming jungles,
digging, cutting, tapping—
striving together for my comfort,
so I could doodle and scratch sentences.
Lord, if so many separate human beings
can work together to produce something
so slight as a pencil,
why can't we work together
to create something more significant,
like universal love or world peace?

Max Pauli

4. THE STRANGER THAT I WAS

Lord, tonight I ask you, once and for all, to
    rid me of my concern
  over what impression I make on other
    people.

Forgive me for being so preoccupied
  with what I seem to be,
  with the effect I produce,
  with what others think and say of me.

Forgive me
  for wanting to imitate others to the extent
    that I forget who I am,
  for envying their talents so much that I
    neglect to develop my own.

Forgive me
  for the time I spend playing games with
    my "personality"
  and for the time I don't spend in
    developing my character.

Now, let me forget about the stranger that
    I was
    so that I may find myself;
    for I will never know my home unless
       I leave it,
    and I will never find myself if I refuse to
       lose myself.

Lord, let me be open to my brothers,
    so that, through them, you will be able to
       visit me as your friend.
For then I will be the person that your Love
       wants me to be,
    your son, Father,
    and a brother to my brothers.

                           Michel Quoist

5. PARAPHRASE OF PSALM 142

I direct my cries to the Lord.
Out of the ear-piercing sounds
   and the ceaseless turmoil
   of this concrete jungle
   I speak God's name.
For my heart is deeply troubled and
      depressed,
   and I feel weary and faint.

I am confused and lost.
I cannot find my way.
The nameless faces that flit by take no
      notice of me.
No one knows my name,
And no one cares.

I turn to you, O God.
You have heard me before,
And you responded to my cries.
Perhaps even amidst the frustrating activity

and the crowded streets of the great
  city
You can hear the cries of a lonely child.

O God, deliver me from my prison of lone-
  liness.
Turn my cries of distress into proclamations
  of joy.
Direct my steps into the fellowship of others
  who love and serve you.

Leslie F. Brandt

*A human being is a mystery which must be
learned slowly, lovingly, with care and
tenderness and pain, and which is never
learned completely.*

Gerald Vann

I don't know what your destiny will be, but one thing I know: the only ones among you who will be really happy are those who have sought and found how to serve.

Albert Schweitzer

VI

Reconciliation
(Private Penance)

"Repent and believe the Good News" (Mk 1:15).

Not only did Jesus ask people to renounce their sins and turn to God. As the good news in the flesh, he personally pardoned sins, poured out his blood for the forgiveness of sins, and authorized his apostles to forgive them.

Baptism is the primary sacrament of conversion and new life in Christ. But since we sin after Baptism—sometimes even gravely—Jesus left his Church the sacrament of Penance. In this sacrament we again turn away from sin, renew our baptismal vows and are reunited to our heavenly Father and our brothers and sisters.

By reflecting on the following we can make our confession more meaningful and fruitful. (Students who do not wish to receive the sacrament of Penance now may wish to use the texts and prayers to ask for God's mercy privately.)

PREPARING FOR CONFESSION

Students should spend time preparing for confession, asking for God's help, reflecting on God's never-failing mercy and forgiveness, and calling to mind the times they have sinned and hence failed to live up to their potential greatness.

Prayer for Light and Courage

God our Father in heaven,
send your Holy Spirit into my heart.
Point out my sins.
Supply the courage I need to confess them
    honestly.
Help me to believe you are always willing
    to forgive.
Remove my sin and guilt,
fill me with peace,
then send me away strong, free,
and determined I will be better in the days
    ahead.
I ask for these things through Jesus, your
    Son,
who is my Lord and Savior.

THE PRODIGAL SON
Lk 15:11-32

Once there was a man who had two sons.
The younger one said to his father, "Father,
give me my share of the property that will
come to me." So he divided up his property
between the two of them. Before very
long, the younger son collected all his
belongings and went off to a foreign land,
where he squandered his wealth in the
wildest extravagance. And when he had
run through all his money, a terrible
famine arose in that country, and he began
to feel the pinch. Then he went and hired
himself out to one of the citizens of that
country who sent him out into the fields to
feed the pigs. He got to the point of
longing to stuff himself with the food the
pigs were eating, and not a soul gave him
anything. Then he came to his senses and
cried aloud, "Why, dozens of my father's
hired men have got more food than they
can eat, and here am I dying of hunger! I
will get up and go back to my father, and
I will say to him: 'Father, I have done
wrong in the sight of heaven and in your
eyes. I don't deserve to be called your
son anymore. Please take me on as one

of your hired men.' " So he got up and went to his father. But while he was still some distance off, his father saw him and his heart went out to him, and he ran and fell on his neck and kissed him. But his son said: "Father, I have done wrong in the sight of heaven and in your eyes. I don't deserve to be called your son any-more. . . ." "Hurry!" called out his father to the servants, "fetch the best clothes and put them on him! Put a ring on his finger and shoes on his feet, and get that calf we've fattened and kill it, and we will have a feast and a celebration! For this is my son—I thought he was dead, and he's alive again. I thought I had lost him, and he's found!" And they began to get the festivities going.

But his elder son was out in the fields, and as he came near the house, he heard music and dancing. So he called one of the servants across to him and inquired what was the meaning of it all. "Your brother has arrived, and your father has killed the calf we fattened because he has got him home again safe and sound," was the reply. But he was furious and refused to go inside the house. So his father came outside and called him. Then he burst out: "Look, how

many years have I slaved for you and never
disobeyed a single order of yours, and yet
you have never given me so much as a
young goat, so that I could give my friends
a dinner! But when that son of yours arrives,
who has spent all your money on
prostitutes, for *him* you kill the calf we've
fattened!" But the father replied: "My dear
son, you have been with me all the time
and everything I have is yours. But we *had*
to celebrate and show our joy. For this is
your brother; I thought he was dead—and
he's alive. I thought he was lost—and he
is found!" (Translation by J. B. Phillips)

EXAMINATION OF CONSCIENCE

"To sin is to break a bond, to destroy a relationship, to withdraw myself from God, my Father, and from his love. . . . A sinful act is less important for the disorder it creates than for what it says about me as a person: Who am I? Whom do I love? What is my attitude toward God?"—W. J. Burghardt, S.J.

I.   The Lord says: "Love the Lord your God with your whole heart."

Do I keep God in mind and put him first in my life? Or am I too caught up in material concerns?
Do I worship God regularly and carefully?
Do I respect his name, or have I dishonored it by using it in anger and carelessness?
Do I pray even when I don't feel like it?
Do I trust God and take seriously enough his personal love and concern for me?
Do I genuinely repent of my sins and accept God's free and gracious forgiveness?

II. The Lord says: "Love one another as I have loved you."

Do I love my parents and brothers and sisters and try to create a happy home life? Or am I sometimes thoughtless or even cruel toward them?

Am I fair and honest in my relationships? Or do I sometimes lie or act phony, or take unfair advantage of others by cheating or stealing?

Am I contributing to the welfare of my school? Or do I ridicule teachers and school officials without trying to make things better?

Do I respect the rights and sensitivities of others? Or do I tend to put people in categories or ignore them because they are different?

Do I honestly try to forgive people who dislike me? Or have I tried to hurt them by what I've said or done?

Am I grateful for my sexuality and anxious to grow in sexual maturity and responsibility? Or do I sometimes exploit members of the opposite sex and use their bodies as playthings?

Am I trying to improve the quality of life around me? Or do I foul up the environment and waste the good things I have?

Do I really care about my country and the good of the human community of which I am a part? Or do I care only about myself and the people I know?

Am I concerned for the poor, the hungry and the destitute and for the millions who thirst for justice and peace?

Can I cut back on excessive eating and drinking and contribute to the poor of the world?

III. Jesus says: "Be perfect as your heavenly Father is perfect."

Am I working at becoming a better person and a better Christian?

Am I making the most of my talents, my education and my opportunities? Or do I fail to use them sometimes?

Do I place knowledge above grades?

Do I take care of my body, and make sure I get enough sleep and exercise?

Do I sometimes eat and drink far too much or misuse my body sexually?

Am I able to admit my own need for help and to ask for it?

Do I accept myself, despite my limitations and weakness?

What is the fundamental orientation of my life?

GOING TO CONFESSION

With the publication of the new Rite of Penance and the renewal of the sacrament, the actual format for confession is flexible. Some students will wish to use a confessional and maintain anonymity as in the past. Other students, desiring a more personal approach, will make an appointment with a priest to confess their sins face to face. In some churches a "reconciliation room" is actually being provided for this procedure. This style of confession allows easy exchange between priest and penitent: for praying together, for reading scripture together, for counsel and advice.

The following directions and prayers are excerpted from the new Rite of Penance for your help and convenience:

Reception of the Penitent

When the penitent comes to confess his sins, the priest welcomes him warmly and greets him with kindness.

Then the penitent makes the sign of the cross which the priest may make also.

In the name of the Father, and of the Son, and of the Holy Spirit. Amen.

The priest invites the penitent to have trust in God, in these or similar words:

May God, who has enlightened every heart,
help you to know your sins
and trust in his mercy.

Or:

The Lord does not wish the sinner to die
but to turn back to him and live.
Come before him with trust in his mercy.
(Ezechiel 33:11)

The penitent answers:

Amen.

Reading of the Word of God (optional)

Then the priest may read or say from memory a text of scripture which proclaims God's mercy and calls man to conversion.

After the confession of sins, with which the priest may help if necessary, the priest proposes a penance which the penitent accepts. The penance may be a prayer or prayers, a reading from scripture, or some more creative penance like an act of charity toward someone the penitent has injured.

Prayer of Sorrow

The priest then asks the penitent to express his sorrow, which the penitent may do in these or similar words:

My God,
I am sorry for my sins with all my heart.
In choosing to do wrong
and failing to do good,
I have sinned against you
whom I should love above all things.
I firmly intend, with your help,
to do penance,
to sin no more,
and to avoid whatever leads me to sin.
Our Savior Jesus Christ
suffered and died for us.
In his name, my God, have mercy.

Or:

Lord Jesus Christ, Son of God,
have mercy on me, a sinner.

Prayer of Absolution

*Then the priest extends his hands over
the penitent's head (or at least extends his
right hand) and says:*

God, the Father of mercies,
through the death and resurrection of
    his Son
has reconciled the world to himself
and sent the Holy Spirit among us
for the forgiveness of sins;
through the ministry of the Church
may God give you pardon and peace,
and I absolve you from your sins
in the name of the Father, and of the Son,+
and of the Holy Spirit.

The penitent answers:

Amen.

Praise of God and Dismissal

After the absolution, the priest continues:

Give thanks to the Lord, for he is good.

The penitent concludes:

His mercy endures for ever.

*Then the priest dismisses the penitent
who has been reconciled, saying:*

The Lord has freed you from your sins. Go
  in peace.

Or:

May the Passion of our Lord Jesus Christ,
the intercession of the Blessed Virgin Mary
    and of all the saints,
whatever good you do and suffering you
    endure,
heal your sins,
help you grow in holiness,
and reward you with eternal life.
Go in peace.

THANKSGIVING AFTER CONFESSION

Almighty and merciful God,
how wonderfully you created us
and still more wonderfully remade us.
You do not abandon the sinner
but seek him out with a father's love.
You sent your Son into the world
to destroy sin and death by his passion,
and to restore life and joy by his resurrection.
You sent the Holy Spirit into our hearts
to make us your children, heirs of your
kingdom.
You constantly renew our spirit
in the sacraments of your redeeming love,
freeing us from slavery to sin
and transforming us ever more
into the image of your beloved Son.
We thank you for the wonders of your
mercy,
and with voice and hand and heart
we join with the whole Church in the new
song of praise.
Glory to you through Christ in the Holy
Spirit,
now and for ever.
Amen.

May the road rise to meet you,
May the wind always be at your back,
May the sun shine warm upon your face,
May the rains fall soft upon your field,
May God hold you in the palm of his hand.

Irish Blessing

VII

Way of the Cross

For centuries the Way of the Cross has been a meaningful devotion for Christians. By isolating various episodes which occurred after Jesus was arrested in the Garden of Gethsemane, we can reflect on his passion, death and resurrection.

Equally important, we can reflect on the fact that the Way of the Cross continues today. There is suffering all around us and we are involved whether we like it or not.

The following Way of the Cross can be prayed by students in their rooms or, better, in a church or chapel where there are stations on the walls which remind us of these episodes.

First Station: Jesus Is Condemned to Death

Jesus is brought before Pilate on trumped-up charges of treason, and is condemned to death.

It's a classic case of injustice, but injustice did not end with the trial of Jesus. As a student, I see injustice all around me. People all over the world are destroyed because of their religion, nationality, or color of their skin.

Furthermore, I see this same kind of injustice in myself—my tendency to put others down or mock them because they are different. In subtle or not-so-subtle ways I do this to my fellow students and others who come from different cultures or different parts of the country, or have strange-sounding names.

Prayer

Help me, Lord, to recognize your features in the features of all I meet so that I do not give way to the injustice of prejudice. Amen.

Second Station: Jesus Accepts His Cross

A heavy cross is thrust into his arms, and he is ordered to carry it to the site of his execution. Jesus accepts the cross with love.

Throughout the world, man is burdened by crosses—war, hunger, poverty. But I seldom realize this. For that matter, I scarcely notice the people around me who are also carrying large crosses: the student who is flunking everything, my grandmother who is nearing the end and is afraid, a friend who is in love with someone who doesn't return that love.

A bad cold, a tough exam, cafeteria food which suddenly seems tasteless, lack of sleep—these are the crosses thrust at me. How do I accept them?

Prayer

Lord, help me to recognize the crosses which others bear. And help me to accept the crosses of my life with the same kind of love with which you accepted your far heavier cross. Amen.

Third Station: Jesus Falls the First Time

The cross is heavy, the road to Calvary is long. Jesus slumps to the ground. Quickly the soldiers drag him to his feet again.

The world is filled with people who have fallen, and are trying desperately to get up. Many are in prisons where conditions are deplorable. Once outside those walls they frequently still are walled in by prejudice toward "ex-cons."

How seldom I realize how precious my freedom is. I have a lifetime ahead of me, come from a good home, and am receiving a good education. There are many paths open to me and I am more or less free to choose the one I want. All this I take for granted while many my age are confined to prison for crimes that I too might have committed. Could it be that my failures are greater than theirs in the eyes of God?

Prayer

Lord, I am often deaf to the cries of those who have fallen. I even look down on them at times and forget about my own failures. Grant that I may be more willing to use my freedom to help those who have none. Amen.

Fourth Station: Jesus Meets His Mother

In horror, Mary watches her son being dragged toward Calvary and certain death.

On our TV screens we have seen the effects of so many wars and natural disasters that we seldom wince. Even the faces of starving children fail to move us now.

This same kind of insensitivity can affect my relationships with those who are close to me. I overlook the pain and discouragement of a fellow student who has been shot down in a test; I fail to see the panic in the eyes of a neighbor whose wife is terminally ill. But when the suffering of another fails to touch me, then I too am suffering from an affliction, and also need to be healed.

Prayer

Lord, your mother looked on your suffering with horror and the deepest love. Grant that I may look on the sufferings of others with true compassion.

Fifth Station:
Simon Helps Jesus Carry the Cross

Because Jesus is faltering under his cross and might die on the way, the soldiers grab a bystander named Simon and order him to help.

We cannot blame Simon for his reluctance to help Jesus. When the faces of poverty, war and despair flood our TV screens, we too look the other way. Who wants to worry about other people's problems? We have enough of our own.

Yet there are things I can do that could help others who are stumbling under their crosses. Within blocks of my school there are kids I could tutor or old folks I could visit. I need to try to get out of myself and move out toward others.

Prayer

Lord, like Simon I turn away from suffering. Help me to be generous enough to share the cross of others who need me.

Sixth Station:
Veronica Wipes the Face of Jesus

As Jesus passes by, a woman of compassion rushes after him and wipes the blood from his face. To her astonishment the outline of his features is left on the cloth.

Veronica still lives today. She lives in someone like Mother Teresa who ministers to the dying derelicts of Calcutta. As Jesus was prepared for death by Veronica, so are the poor prepared for death by Mother Teresa and her followers.

I may never see India but there are opportunities in my life for a kind word, a compassionate gesture. Without being phony I can support and encourage a friend who is having a bad day. I can do some typing for someone bogged down by a long term paper. There are all sorts of ways I can help.

Prayer

Lord, help me to realize that showing compassion to another person need not involve a trip across the world. The opportunities are present everywhere.

Seventh Station: Jesus Falls the Second Time

Despite Simon's assistance, Jesus again falls. He lies sprawling on the ground until the soldiers roughly pull him to his feet again.

The weight of the cross and his own weakness forced Jesus to the ground. Oppression and greed force many to their knees in our society. Perhaps the most disadvantaged segment of our population, for example, is the farm worker who frequently is grossly underpaid and lives in shacks. Yet his efforts to improve his conditions have been resisted for decades and still are rebuffed today.

I find it easy to overlook the burden which forces strangers to the ground. I am well-fed, well-housed and well-educated. But are not these strangers my brothers and sisters?

Prayer

Lord, so often I am blind to the needs of others—especially when they are strangers. Remove my blindness and increase my love.

Eighth Station:
Jesus Speaks to the Weeping Women

Forgetting about his own pain, Jesus consoles women who are weeping at his condition.

Overwhelmed by grief, the women could do nothing but weep when they saw Jesus. But tears are not enough. If we reflect on the millions who are facing death by starvation around the world, we may also feel like crying. But tears do not produce bread.

To help the starving I must do my part. This means studying the problem and searching out long-range solutions. It also means that I should try to "live with" those who are starving by cutting down on food or by fasting occasionally. And it means I should give my support and prayers to agencies and persons who are carrying food and ideas to the hungry.

Prayer

Lord, help me not simply to weep over the suffering like the women did over you; help me to do whatever I can to feed the hungry millions of the world.

Ninth Station: Jesus Falls the Third Time

Lack of sleep, the scourging and crowning with thorns, the horrible journey with his cross—all have taken their toll. Once more Jesus slumps to the ground.

Failure. Millions live constantly with a numbing sense of their own failures. The alcoholic reaching for a bottle, and hating himself for it; the drug addict who is destroying himself; students who are overwhelmed by sexual experiences which bring them only guilt and shame.

"I can't go on." Sometimes I feel that way. There's a test coming and I'm facing another "all nighter" at the books. Or I become painfully aware of my own weaknesses and shortcomings and get down on myself. I need the courage to keep getting back up on my feet.

Prayer

Lord, I'm like millions of others—I find it difficult to keep trying to do my best. I get discouraged at my failures. Please give me the courage I need to get back up like you did.

Tenth Station:
Jesus Is Stripped of His Garments

The journey comes to an end at Calvary. The soldiers quickly strip away his clothes, leaving him naked in front of the crowd.

A poor man, Jesus is stripped of the little that is his. Today the same process continues on a massive scale. Wealthy nations like ours scoop up larger and larger amounts of the world's goods while the poorer nations get poorer.

I am conscious of all that I have—my clothes, stereo, enough money to keep me supplied with extras. I may not like to admit it, but these possessions mean a lot to me. Is it possible for me to "strip" myself of some of my worldly goods and share them with others not so fortunate?

Prayer

Lord, I am very selfish. I cling to everything I own. Help me to place less importance on material things and to share what has been given me.

Eleventh Station:
Jesus Is Nailed to the Cross

Roughly the soldiers hurl Jesus down on the cross he has been carrying. Then they nail his hands and feet to the wood.

The soldiers who nailed Jesus to the cross have their counterparts today. In some countries, torture and brutality are part of the governing process. Political prisoners are beaten, receive electrical shocks, are brutally brainwashed. Seldom does our government, or its citizens, protest strongly.

Torture has various forms. I know a few of my own. I can make another student wince by the mocking word, the clever cut. I know how to irritate my parents or stir up an argument with a brother or sister. Pass the nails, please.

Prayer

Lord, torture is an ugly word. Help me to combat its use throughout the world if I can. Above all, help me to root it out of my own life so that I no longer nail people to crosses by word or action.

Twelfth Station: Jesus Dies on the Cross

The nightmare of pain and suffering comes to an end. After three hours on the cross, Jesus dies.

Death by violence. His was not the first and certainly not the last. In our cities each day dozens are fatally shot and knifed, beaten to death in fights, wiped out in senseless traffic accidents. And then there is institutional violence, caused by the fact that a privileged few of us control most of the earth's resources and can cheerfully watch the poor scramble for the crumbs we leave behind. Many die before they get them.

I don't think much about death, and not at all about my own death. It's such a painful topic and, besides, I have many years ahead of me if my luck holds out. Or is it fear that makes me reluctant to think about it? I need to get in touch with the feelings I have about death so that I can use my life well.

Prayer

Lord, I confess that I fear death and don't like to face the fact that one day I shall die. Please give me courage to live my days well and to die my death with you at my side.

Thirteenth Station:
Jesus Is Taken Down from the Cross

His body hangs limply. The soldiers cut him down and place him, bleeding and broken, in the arms of his mother.

The scene is repeated constantly: A mother receives the body of a son or husband slain in another senseless war. It makes no difference where the war is fought or the color of the skin of the participants— the grief is the same. Incredibly, the wars continue and the grief mounts. Another mother today will receive the broken body of her son.

I feel helpless in the face of grief like this. I feel helpless, too, when a neighbor dies, or the mother or father of a friend. What can I possibly say or do that would help? Really there is nothing I can say or do, except to stand by those who are grieving and to make their grief my own. I cannot cure their grief, but I can care.

Prayer

Lord, with infinite gentleness your mother took your body into her arms after your death. Grant me the same kind of gentleness so that I may comfort those who are grieving.

Fourteenth Station: The Burial of Jesus

Relatives and friends carry his body to the grave. They place it inside, roll a boulder across the entrance, and silently withdraw.

The suffering of Calvary still continues. We can see it in the faces of the hungry and destitute of the world, in the victims of war and disaster. Yes, we can see suffering in the eyes of those around us—even in the eyes of our own families and friends.

Our response? Because we are young we have the hope that tomorrow will be better. To make it so we need skills, training and the best utilization of our own God-given talents. But we must never forget that we also have to bury our own selfishness, our own insensitivity.

Only then can we help those who are looking to us and calling our names.

Prayer

Lord, when you were buried it seemed like the end of everything you promised and stood for. But it wasn't, it was only the beginning. Help me to bury my own selfishness as the beginning of a stronger love for you and your people.

EPILOGUE: The Resurrection

On the first Easter morning the friends and relatives of Jesus learn the incredible Good News: Jesus has risen from the dead; he has overcome death.

The Way of the Cross spotlights the dark side of mankind and the dark side of ourselves. But there can be no despair—the resurrection sees to that!

Jesus' resurrection reminds us that all suffering and pain (our own and others') is worthwhile and somehow makes sense.

It also reminds us that each one of us is a special gift. We are redeemed! Accepted as we are by our Redeemer, we certainly ought to be able to accept ourselves.

Finally, the resurrection reminds us that our lives are supremely worthwhile and that the "worthwhileness" is measured by the way we love one another.

As students we can learn to be healers and not destroyers. Right now we can minister to the needs of those around us, and those far away.

Prayer

Lord, you have given me talents and gifts. Help me to use them in your service and in the service of my neighbor.

VIII

The Rosary of the Blessed Virgin Mary

The Rosary is a way of meditating on the meaning of Jesus' life, death and resurrection. Its 15 mysteries are arranged in groups of five and follow the historical sequence of his life and that of his blessed mother. Each decade of the Rosary is made up of one Our Father, ten Hail Marys and one Glory. The constant repetition of the same vocal prayers and the use of Rosary beads help set up a rhythm favorable to peaceful, recollected prayer.

Many people use one or more of the following methods to help concentrate on the mysteries:

1. Read one of the bible passages suggested below before each decade;
2. Add a suitable phrase to the first half of the Hail Mary each time it is said;
3. Make an extemporaneous meditation before each decade.

THE JOYFUL MYSTERIES

1. The Annunciation of the Angel Gabriel
    to Mary   Luke 1:26-38/ Isaiah 7:10-14

    *Hail, Mary, . . . and blessed is the fruit of
    your womb, Jesus, who was conceived
    at the message of an angel.*

2. The Visitation of Mary to Elizabeth
    Luke 1:39-45/ John 1:19-23/ Isaiah 40:1-10

    *Hail, Mary, . . . the fruit of your womb,
    Jesus, who sanctified the Baptist in the
    womb of his mother.*

3. The Birth of Jesus in Bethlehem of Judea
    Luke 2:1-20/ Matthew 2:1-12/
    Micah 5:1-5/ Galatians 4:1-7

    *Hail, Mary, . . . the fruit of your womb,
    Jesus, who was born for us in the stable
    of Bethlehem.*

4. The Presentation of Christ in the Temple
    Luke 2:22-32/ Hebrews 9:6-14

    *Hail, Mary, . . . the fruit of your womb,
    Jesus, the glory of your people Israel.*

5: The Finding of Christ in the Temple
Luke 2:41-50/ 1 Corinthians 2:6-16/
John 12:44-50

Hail, Mary, . . . the fruit of your womb, Jesus, the power and the wisdom of God.

THE SORROWFUL MYSTERIES

1. The Agony of Jesus in the Garden of Gethsemane   Matthew 26:36-46/
Mark 14:26-42/ Luke 22:39-53/
John 18:1-12

Hail, Mary, . . . the fruit of your womb, Jesus, who sweat blood in the garden of Gethsemane.

2. The Scourging of Jesus at the Pillar
Matthew 27:15-26/ Mark 16:6-16/
Isaiah 50:5-9

Hail, Mary, . . . the fruit of your womb, Jesus, who was bruised for our offenses.

3. The Crowning of Jesus with Thorns
Matthew 27:27-31/ Mark 15:16-19/

Luke 23:6-11/ John 19:1-7/
Isaiah 52:13-53:10/ Matthew 16:24-28

*Hail, Mary, . . . the fruit of your womb,
Jesus, a man of sorrows and acquainted
with grief.*

4. The Way of the Cross   Mark 16:20-25/
John 19:17-22/ Philippians 2:6-11/
Mark 8:31-38

*Hail, Mary, . . . the fruit of your womb,
Jesus, who was crushed for our sins.*

5. The Crucifixion and Death of Jesus
Mark 15:33-39/ John 19:17-37/
Hebrews 9:11-14/ Acts 22:22-24

*Hail, Mary, . . . the fruit of your womb,
Jesus, by whose wounds we are healed.*

THE GLORIOUS MYSTERIES

1. The Resurrection of Christ from the
Dead   Mark 16:1-8/ Matthew 28:1-10/
Luke 24:1-11/ John 20:1-10/
1 Corinthians 15:1-11/ Romans 6:1-14

Hail, Mary, . . . the fruit of your womb,

Jesus, who died for our sins and rose for our justification.

2. The Ascension of Christ into Heaven
   Matthew 28:16-20/ Luke 24:44-53/
   Acts 1:1-11/ Ephesians 2:4-7

   Hail, Mary, . . . the fruit of your womb, Jesus, who now sits at the right hand of the Father.

3. The Gift of the Holy Spirit: Pentecost
   Acts 2:1-11/ Acts 4:23-31/ Acts 11:44-48/
   John 14:15-21

   Hail, Mary, . . . the fruit of your womb, Jesus, who bequeathed us the Holy Spirit as he had promised.

4. The Falling Asleep and Assumption of
   Our Lady   Revelations 21:1-6/
   John 11:17-27/ 1 Corinthians 15:20-28/
   1 Corinthians 15:42-50/
   1 Corinthians 15:51-57

   Hail, Mary, . . . the fruit of your womb, Jesus, who makes all things new.

5. The Coronation of Our Lady and the
   Glory of All the Saints   Revelation 21:1-6/
   Revelation 7:1-4, 9-12/ Matthew 5:1-12

   Hail, Mary, . . . the fruit of your womb, Jesus, who will come again in glory with all his saints.

IX

The Jesus Prayer

One of the oldest, simplest and best of prayers is a calling in faith upon the Holy Name of Jesus. By repeatedly invoking the proper name of Our Lord, God and Savior, Jesus Christ, Christians are convinced that they will be enabled to penetrate more and more deeply and surely into a growing awareness of the presence of God that saves and sanctifies. The sacred name is sometimes repeated by itself or sometimes inserted in a phrase. The common form of the fuller invocation is:

LORD JESUS CHRIST,
SON OF THE LIVING GOD,
HAVE MERCY ON ME, A SINNER.

The best way to say the Jesus Prayer is to sit in as much physical and inner stillness as one can manage and to repeat the invocation over and over, slowly and insistently, fixing the mind directly and intensely on the words of the prayer itself, without trying to conjure up any mental pictures or intellectual concepts. One should pray in this way without strain but with real effort for some length of time at each attempt.

A rosary is a useful timer and reminder in this effort. Persistent, frequent attempts to pray in this way will gradually habituate the soul to more effortless and continuous use of the Divine Name until it becomes the very substance of one's life of prayer. It is well to use the Holy Name insistently and quietly before and after other forms of prayer. It can also be used during normal intervals in the day's work, when walking from place to place, and so forth, even when conditions are not ideal for recollected forms of prayer.

Great saints and fervent mystics tell us that the Jesus Prayer can even become self-acting as it descends from the lips and mind into the heart, the very center of a person's being. Such a gift comes as a pure grace, but as one that can and should be prepared for by genuine effort and serious habituation in the first place.

The Jesus Prayer is a high act of faith and self-surrender to the indwelling Spirit who longs to teach us to pray without ceasing to Abba, our heavenly Father. It is a sure path to contemplative prayer and to "the peace which passes all understanding."

"Jesus is honey to the mouth, music to the ear, a shout of gladness in the heart" (St. Bernard of Clairvaux).

X

Morning and Evening Prayer

Our Lord prayed every day—morning and evening. He was a good Jew who had learned from his mother how to sanctify and dedicate his days and nights to his heavenly Father.

Let us pray daily with him and in him, in union with our brothers and sisters all over the world.

SUNDAY MORNING

Blessed be the kingdom of the Father, and
of the Son, and of the Holy Spirit,
—now and forever. Amen.

Te Deum

You are God: we praise you;
　　You are the Lord: we acclaim you;
You are the eternal Father:
　　All creation worships you.

To you all angels, all the powers of heaven,
　　Cherubim and Seraphim, sing in end-
　　　　less praise:
Holy, holy, holy Lord, God of power and
　　might,
　　heaven and earth are full of your glory.

The glorious company of apostles praise
　　　　you.
　　The noble fellowship of prophets
　　praise you.
　　The white-robed army of martyrs praise
　　you.

Throughout the world the holy Church
        acclaims you:
    Father, of majesty unbounded,
your true and only Son, worthy of all
        worship,
        and the Holy Spirit, advocate and guide.

You, Christ, are the king of glory,
        eternal Son of the Father.
When you became man to set us free
        you did not spurn the Virgin's womb.

You overcame the sting of death
        and opened the kingdom of heaven to
        all believers.
You are seated at God's right hand in glory.
        We believe that you will come, and be
        our judge.

Come then, Lord, help your people,
        bought with the price of your own
        blood,
and bring us with your saints
        to glory everlasting.

Collect Prayer

Only-begotten Son and Word of God,
for our salvation you took flesh of the
    Virgin Mary
and came to live among us as a man;
you were crucified and you destroyed
    death by your death,
and rose again on the third day.
Forgive us our sins and sanctify us to
    your service,
for you are the happiness and joy of
    those who love you,
O Savior of the world,
living and reigning with the Father and
    the Holy Spirit,
now and forever.
Amen.

Reading   Mk 16:5-6

On entering the tomb the women saw a
young man in a white robe seated on the
right-hand side, and they were struck with
amazement. But he said to them, "There is
no need for alarm. You are looking for
Jesus of Nazareth, who was crucified: he
has risen, he is not here. See, here is the
place where they laid him."

Response

Arise, O Christ, and help us,
—and deliver us for your name's sake.

Morning Prayer

Father of glory,
you raised Jesus Christ from the dead
and made him sit at your right hand.
Rescue us from our sins, bring us to
new life in him,
and give us a place with him in heaven,
in the same Christ Jesus our Lord.
Amen.

Apostles' Creed   **Lord's Prayer**

May the God of Abraham, Isaac and Jacob,
May the God of Peter, James and John,
May the God of us all bless us
in the name of the Father, Son and Holy
Spirit.
Amen.

Heritage Blessing

SUNDAY EVENING

Light and peace in Jesus Christ our Lord.
—Thanks be to God.

Canticle of the Blessed Virgin Mary Lk 1:46-55

Ant.   Happy are those who hear the word
of God and keep it. (Lk 11:28)

My soul proclaims the greatness of the Lord,
my spirit rejoices in God my Savior;
for he has looked with favor on his lowly
servant.
From this day all generations will
call me blessed:

The Almighty has done great things for me:
holy is his name.
He has mercy on those who fear him
in every generation.

He has shown the strength of his arm,
he has scattered the proud in their
conceit.
He has cast down the mighty from their
thrones,
and has lifted up the lowly.
He has filled the hungry with good things,
and the rich he has sent away empty.

He has come to the help of his servant
>Israel,
>for he remembered his promise of
>mercy,
the promise he made to our fathers,
>to Abraham and his children for ever.

Glory to the Father, and to the Son, and to
>the Holy Spirit:
>as it was in the beginning, is now, and
>will be for ever. Amen.

Collect Prayer

>Lord Jesus Christ,
>in your suffering you cried out to your
>Father
>and he delivered you out of death.
>By the power of your life-giving cross,
>rescue us from the abyss of sin,
>renew this world of yours in peace
>and flood our minds with the light of
>your resurrection,
>O Savior of the world,
>living and reigning for ever and ever.
>Amen.

Reading I Cor 15:3-8

I taught you what I had been taught
myself, namely, that Christ died for our sins,
in accordance with the scriptures; that he
was buried; and that he was raised to life
on the third day, in accordance with
the scriptures; that he appeared first to
Cephas and secondly to the Twelve. Next
he appeared to more than five hundred of
the brothers at the same time, most of
whom are still alive, though some have
died; then he appeared to James, and then
to all the apostles; and last of all he
appeared to me too.

Response

> Give thanks to God the Father always
>   and for everything
> —in the name of our Lord Jesus Christ.

Evening Prayer

> Lord Jesus Christ,
> faithful witness and first-born from the
>   dead,
> ruler of the kings of the earth,
> wash away our sins in your blood

and make us a line of kings and priests
to serve your God and Father;
to him be honor and glory for ever
    and ever.
Amen.

Lord's Prayer   **Hail Mary**

In Praise of the Trinity

To God the Father,
who loved us and made us accepted in the
    Beloved:
To God the Son,
who loved us and loosed us from our sins
    by his own blood:
To God the Holy Spirit,
who sheds the love of God abroad in our
    hearts:
To the one true God,
be all love and glory for time and for
    eternity.
Amen.

Bishop Thomas Ken

MONDAY MORNING

Our help is in the name of the Lord
—who made heaven and earth.

The Song of the Three Young Men
(Dn 3:52-56)

Ant. Let us praise the Lord, the God of
Israel. (Lk 1:68)

Blessed are you, O Lord, God of our fathers,
    praised and glorified above all for ever.
Blessed be your glorious and holy name,
    praised and glorified above all for ever.
Blessed are you in the temple of your
        sacred glory,
    praised and glorified above all for ever.
Blessed are you on the throne of your
        kingdom,
    praised and glorified above all for ever.
Blessed are you enthroned on the cherubim,
    praised and glorified above all for ever.
Blessed are you who look into the depths,
    praised and glorified above all for ever.
Blessed are you in the heavenly vault,
    praised and glorified above all for ever.
Blessed be the Father, the Son and the Holy
        Spirit,
    praised and glorified above all for ever.

Collect Prayer

>Almighty God and Father,
>all creation speaks eloquently of your
>   wonderful works.
>Let your glory shine forth in our lives
>that everything we say and do
>may praise you in union with all the
>   saints,
>in the name of Jesus Christ our Lord.
>Amen.

Reading   Mt 11:28-30

Come to me, all you who labor and are overburdened, and I will give you rest. Shoulder my yoke and learn from me, for I am gentle and humble of heart, and you will find rest for your souls. Yes, my yoke is easy and my burden light.

Response

>In the morning you hear me;
>—in the morning I offer you my prayer.

Morning Prayer

Lord God almighty,
you are the beginning and the end,
    the first and the last;
direct our hearts and bodies
in the love of God and the patience of
    Christ;
bless us, defend us from all evil
and bring us in safety to life everlasting;
we ask this through Christ our Lord.
Amen.

Apostles' Creed   Lord's Prayer

*The Christian must remember that he is
likely to be the only copy of the gospels that
the non-Christian will ever see.*
                                        Philip Scharper

MONDAY EVENING

Light and peace in Jesus Christ our Lord.
—Thanks be to God.

Psalm 113

Ant.　He has cast down the mighty from
　　　their thrones and lifted up the lowly.
　　　(Lk 1:52)

You servants of the Lord,
　　praise his name!
His name will be praised,
　　now and forever!
From the east to the west,
　　the Lord's name be praised!
The Lord rules over all nations,
　　his glory is above the heavens.

There is no one like the Lord our God;
　　he lives in the heights above,
but he bends down
　　to see the heavens and the earth.
He raises the poor from the dust;
　　he lifts the needy from their misery,
and makes them companions of princes,
　　the princes of his people.

Glory to the Father, and to the Son, and to
the Holy Spirit:
as it was in the beginning, is now, and
will be for ever. Amen.

Psalm Prayer

Lord our God,
your name is praised from sunrise to
sunset
because of your loving providence and
constant care;
make us worthy to thank you for your
great glory
through Jesus Christ our Lord.
Amen.

Reading   Col 3:16-17
Let the message of Christ, in all its
richness, find a home with you. Teach
each other, and advise each other, in
all wisdom. With gratitude in your
hearts sing psalms and hymns and inspired songs to God; and never say
or do anything except in the name of
the Lord Jesus, giving thanks to God
the Father through him.

Response

> Guard me as the apple of your eye, O
>   Lord.
> —Hide me in the shadow of your
>   wings.

Evening Prayer

> Lighten our darkness, O Lord,
> and by your great mercy
> defend us from all perils and dangers
> of this night,
> for the love of your only Son, our
>   Savior Jesus Christ.
> Amen.

Lord's Prayer   **Hail Mary**

*May the Lord preserve in us all a passionate
zest for the world, much gentleness, and
may he help us be more fully human to
the end.*

                    Teilhard de Chardin

TUESDAY MORNING

*Holy is God, holy and mighty, holy and
        living for ever.*
    —Lord, have mercy on us.

The Song of the Three Young Men
(Dn 3:57-73)

Ant.   Creation eagerly awaits the full
    revelation of God in Christ. (Rm 8:19)

Bless the Lord, sing to his glory,
    all things fashioned by his mighty hand;
Praise his strength, sing to his name,
    in the present age and in eternity.

Praise the Lord, all you holy angels,
        who assist with reverence at his holy
            throne.
Let the blue skies bless the Lord,
        and all that the heavenly sphere em-
            braces.
Bless the Lord, all you waters,
        which reside above the heavens;
All the great powers of the Lord,
        sing his praises for ever.
Let the sun and moon bless the Lord,
        they whose rays put to flight the dark-
            ness.

Let the great and brilliant stars
  give their light to praise God's great-
    ness.
Bless the Lord, all heavenly dew,
  bless the Lord, every drop of moisture.
Bless the Lord, all mighty winds,
  you ministers of his majesty.

Bless the Lord, all fire and heat,
  which dry the earth in summertime.
Bless the Lord, all icy blasts,
  which bring snow and ice in winter.
Bless the Lord, all mists and frosts,
  which crown the peaks of mountains.
Let each day and night of the year
  and changing seasons bless the Lord.
Bless the Lord at all times,
  both in the morning and in the evening.
And may the dark clouds bless the Lord,
  through the terror of the lightning.
Let us praise the Father, the Son and the
    Holy Spirit,
  one blessed Trinity, now and for ever.

Collect Prayer

  Lord God, creator of heaven and of
    earth,
  you fashioned the human powers of
    reason and of speech

and set us apart to sing your praises.
Accept our hymns of praise which we
offer you
in union with all that you have made,
for all the powers of heaven glorify you,
Father, Son and Holy Spirit,
now and for ever.
Amen.

Reading   Mt 10:32-33

If anyone declares himself for me in the
presence of men, I will declare myself for
him in the presence of my Father in heaven.
But the one who disowns me in the
presence of men, I will disown in the
presence of my Father in heaven.

Response

Send forth your light and your truth;
—let these be my guide.

Morning Prayer

Lord our God,
your power is beyond all words to
describe,
your glory is measureless,

your mercy is without limits
and your love for us is beyond all
    telling;
in your kindness grant to us
and to all those praying with us
the riches of your compassion and
    mercy;
grant this through Christ our Lord.
Amen.

Apostles' Creed   **Lord's Prayer**

Prayer does not blind us to the world,
but it transforms our vision of the world,
and makes us see it, all men,
and all the history of mankind,
in the light of God.

                              Thomas Merton

TUESDAY EVENING

Jesus Christ is the light of the world,
—a light no darkness can extinguish.

Psalm 121

Ant.   You should be awake and praying
         not to be put to the test. (Mk 14:38)

I look to the mountains;
     where will my help come from?
My help comes from the Lord,
     who made heaven and earth.

May he not let me fall;
     may my protector keep awake!
The protector of Israel
     does not doze or sleep!

The Lord will guard you;
     he is by your side to protect you.
The sun will not hurt you during the day,
     nor the moon during the night.

The Lord will protect you from all danger;
     he will keep you safe.
He will protect you as you come and go,
     from now on and forever.

Glory to the Father, and to the Son, and to
the Holy Spirit:
as it was in the beginning, is now, and
will be for ever. Amen.

Psalm Prayer

Maker of heaven and earth,
unsleeping guardian of your faithful
people,
protect us both by day and by night
from the obstacles
which the world, the flesh and the
devil put in our path;
we ask this through Christ our Lord.
Amen.

Reading   Rm 12:1-2

Think of God's mercy and worship him, I
beg you, in a way that is worthy of thinking
beings, by offering your living bodies as a
holy sacrifice, truly pleasing to God. Do not
model yourselves on the behavior of the
world around you, but let your behavior
change, modeled by your new mind. This
is the only way to discover the will of God
and know what is good, what it is that God
wants, what is the perfect thing to do.

Response

Though I walk in darkness,
—the Lord is my light.

Evening Prayer

Lord Jesus Christ,
as evening falls to end another day,
may the sunshine of your saving
        presence
go on shining in our hearts,
and put to flight the threatening gloom
        of sin and danger;
you live and reign for ever and ever.
Amen.

Lord's Prayer   **Hail Mary**

*If you love the good that you see in another,
you make it your own.*
                    St. Gregory the Great

WEDNESDAY MORNING

*Blessed be the Lord, our God, the King of
    the universe,*
—now and for ever. Amen.

The Song of the Three Young Men
(Dn 3:57, 74-81)

Ant.   Creation itself shares the glorious
    freedom of the children of God. (Rm
    8:21)

Bless the Lord, sing to his glory,
    all things fashioned by his mighty hand;
Praise his strength, sing to his name,
    in the present age and in eternity.
Let the earth and all that is in it
    praise the greatness of the Lord.
Let the towering mountains bless the Lord,
    with the forests and the lowly hills.
Let the flowers and the plants bless the Lord,
    every growing thing earth yields.
Bless the Lord, all flowing fountains,
    which spring from far below the earth.
Bless the Lord, seas and rivers,
    whose waters carry the ships of men.
Bless the Lord, you fish and sea monsters,
    all creatures living in the waters.

Bless the Lord, all you winged creatures,
    who fly the heavens majestically.
Bless the Lord, all you animals,
    those which are wild and those which
        serve us.
Let us praise the Father, the Son and the
    Holy Spirit,
    one blessed Trinity, now and forever.

Collect Prayer

    Lord God, creator of heaven and earth,
    planet earth is made to reveal your
        loving-kindness
    and to support the human race in
        dignity and peace.
    Teach us to praise you as you deserve
    in union with all the splendors of your
        creation,
    through Jesus Christ our Lord and
        Brother.
    Amen.

Reading   Mt 16:24-26

Jesus said to his disciples, "If anyone wants
to be a follower of mine, let him renounce
himself and take up his cross and follow me.
For anyone who wants to save his life will

lose it; but anyone who loses his life for my sake will find it. What, then, will a man gain if he wins the whole world and ruins his life? Or what has a man to offer in exchange for his life?"

Response

O God, you are my God,
—for you I long from early morning.

Morning Prayer

Lord God, King of heaven and earth,
direct and sanctify, rule and guide
our hearts and bodies, our thoughts,
    words and deeds
in the doing of your law and the keep-
    ing of your commandments,
so that today and every day we may
    be kept safe and free,
O Savior of the world,
living and reigning for ever and ever.
Amen.

Apostles' Creed   **Lord's Prayer**

WEDNESDAY EVENING

I am the light of the world,
—whoever follows me will have the light
   of life.

Psalm 134

Ant.   Jesus spent the whole night in prayer.
   (Lk 6:12)

Come, praise the Lord,
   all his servants,
   all who serve in his temple at night.
Raise your hands in prayer in the temple,
   and praise the Lord!

May the Lord, who made heaven and earth,
   bless you from Zion.

Glory to the Father, and to the Son, and to
      the Holy Spirit:
   as it was in the beginning, is now, and
      will be forever. Amen.

Psalm Prayer

Father almighty, to whom saints and
      angels sing,
   clothe us in the mantle of praise

that we may rejoice in proclaiming
your glory
and in receiving your blessings;
we ask this in the name of Jesus our
Lord.
Amen.

Reading Eph 6:11, 14-17

Put God's armor on so as to be able to re-
sist the devil's tactics. . . . Stand your
ground, with truth buckled round your
waist, and integrity for a breastplate, wear-
ing for shoes on your feet the eagerness to
spread the gospel of peace and always
carrying the shield of faith so that you can
use it to put out the burning arrows of the
evil one. And then you must accept salvation from God to be your helmet and receive the word of God from the Spirit to use
as a sword.

Response

It is good to give thanks to the Lord,
—to proclaim your truth in the watches
of the night.

Evening Prayer

Look down, O Lord, from your
heavenly throne,
illuminate the darkness of this coming
night
with your celestial brightness,
and from the children of light banish
the deeds of darkness;
grant this through Christ our Lord.
Amen.

Lord's Prayer   **Hail Mary**

*Do what you can and then pray that God
will give you the power to do what you
cannot.*

St. Augustine

THURSDAY MORNING

*Glory to God in the highest
and peace to your people on earth.*

The Song of the Three Young Men
(Dn 3:57, 82-88)

Ant. You are a chosen race, a royal priest-
hood, a consecrated nation, a people
set apart to sing the praises of God.
(1 Pt 2:9)

Bless the Lord, sing to his glory,
all things fashioned by his mighty hand;
Praise his strength, sing to his name,
in the present age and in eternity.

Let the human race do all within its power
to extol the glory of God's name.
Bless the Lord all you human creatures,
and praise his goodness eternally.
O Israel, bless your God continually,
for ever and ever praise his greatness.
Bless the Lord all you his priests;
bless him faithfully, all you his servants.
Bless the Lord all you holy souls;
you who are humble love him.

Let everyone sing to God's glory and praise
       him,
    from the present moment unto eternity.
Let us praise the Father, the Son and the
       Holy Spirit,
    one blessed Trinity, now and for ever.

Collect Prayer

    Holy God and Father,
    as you rest among the saints,
    the seraphim praise you, the cherubim
       sing your glory,
    and all the powers of heaven and earth
       fall down before you.
    Allow us to stand in your holy presence
    and to offer you the praise and worship
       you deserve
    in union with the whole company of
       heaven;
    we ask this through the merits of Jesus
       Christ our Savior.
    Amen.

Reading   Mt 20:25-28

Jesus called his disciples to him and said,
"You know that among the pagans the
rulers lord it over them, and their great
men make their authority felt. This is not

to happen among you. No; anyone who
wants to be great among you must be your
servant, and anyone who wants to be first
among you must be your slave, just as the
Son of Man came not to be served but to
serve, and to give his life as a ransom for
many."

Response

In you is the source of life, O Lord,
—and in your light we see light.

Morning Prayer

Almighty God and Father,
unto whom all hearts are open, all
        desires known
and from whom no secrets are hidden,
cleanse the thoughts of our hearts
by the inspiration of your Holy Spirit,
that we may perfectly love you
and worthily praise your holy name;
we ask this through Christ our Lord.
Amen.

Apostles' Creed   **Lord's Prayer**

THURSDAY EVENING

Light and peace in Jesus Christ our Lord.
—Thanks be to God.

Psalm 138

Ant. The Word of God is the King of
kings and the Lord of lords. (Rv 19:16)

I thank you, Lord, with all my heart;
I sing praise to you before the angels.
I bow down in front of your holy temple
and praise your name,
because of your constant love and faithfulness,
because you have shown that you and your
commands are supreme.
You answered me when I called to you;
with your strength you strengthened
me.

All the kings of the earth will praise you,
Lord,
because they have heard your promises.
They will sing about what the Lord has
done,
and about his great glory.
Even though the Lord is so high above,

he cares for the lowly,
and the proud cannot hide from him.

Even when I am surrounded by troubles,
you keep me safe;
you oppose my angry enemies,
and save me by your power.
You will do everything you have promised
me;
Lord, your love is constant forever.
Complete the work that you have
begun.

Glory to the Father, and to the Son, and to
the Holy Spirit:
as it was in the beginning, is now, and
will be for ever. Amen.

Psalm Prayer

Holy Father,
you raised the Lord Jesus to life
and frustrated his mortal foes.
Raise us with Jesus in our turn
and set us by his side in the presence
of the angels;
we ask this through the same Christ
our Lord.
Amen.

Reading   Col 3:12-13

You are God's chosen race, his saints; he loves you, and you should be clothed in sincere compassion, in kindness and humility, gentleness and patience. Bear with one another; forgive each other as soon as a quarrel begins. The Lord has forgiven you; now you must do the same.

Response

> The Lord is my light and my salvation.
> —Whom shall I fear?

Morning Prayer

> Hear our prayers, O Lord,
> and protect us both by night and by
>   day,
> that whatever the changes and chances
>   of this mortal life,
> we may always find strength in your
>   unchanging love;
> we ask this through Jesus our Lord.
> Amen.

Lord's Prayer   **Hail Mary**

FRIDAY MORNING

*Come, let us worship Christ, our King and
    our God,*
—and bow down before him.

Canticle of Zachary (Lk 1:67-79)

Ant. Let us thank God for giving us the
    victory through our Lord Jesus Christ.
    (1 Cor 15:57)

Blessed be the Lord, the God of Israel;
    he has come to his people and set
        them free.
He has raised up for us a mighty savior,
    born of the house of his servant David.

Through his holy prophets he promised of
    old
    that he would save us from our
        enemies,
    from the hands of all who hate us.
He promised to show mercy to our fathers
    and to remember his holy covenant.
This was the oath he swore to our father
    Abraham:
    to set us free from the hands of our
        enemies,
free to worship him without fear,
    holy and righteous in his sight
    all the days of our life.

You, my child, shall be called the prophet
of the Most High,
for you will go before the Lord to
prepare his way,
to give his people knowledge of salvation
by forgiveness of their sins.

In the tender compassion of our God
the dawn from on high shall break
upon us,
to shine on those who dwell in darkness
and the shadow of death,
and to guide our feet on the road to
peace.

Glory to the Father, and to the Son, and to
the Holy Spirit:
as it was in the beginning, is now, and
will be for ever. Amen.

Collect Prayer

Lord Jesus Christ,
you loved us and offered yourself up
for us
as an agreeable and fragrant sacrifice to
God.
Deliver us from our former darkness
and teach us to conduct ourselves as

children of the light
in all goodness, justice and truth;
you live and reign for ever and ever.
Amen.

Reading Mk 10:32-34

Taking the Twelve aside Jesus began to tell
them what was going to happen to him:
"Now we are going up to Jerusalem, and
the Son of Man is about to be handed over
to the chief priests and the scribes. They
will condemn him to death and will hand
him over to the pagans, who will mock him
and spit at him and scourge him and put
him to death; and after three days he will
rise again."

Response

We adore you, O Christ, and we bless
    you,
—for by your holy cross you have re-
    deemed the world.

Morning Prayer

God of mercy and compassion,
long-suffering in the face of our
    wickedness,

blot out our sins by the power of the
cross,
and free us from the assaults of the
evil one
by the grace of your Holy Spirit;
we ask this through Jesus Christ our
Lord.
Amen.

Apostles' Creed   **Lord's Prayer**

*The tragedy of life is what dies inside a
man while he lives.*

Albert Schweitzer

Three O'Clock Prayer

We adore your cross, O Lord, and we praise
 and glorify your holy resurrection, for
 by the wood of the cross joy came into
 the whole world.

My God, the sons of men find refuge
 in the shadow of your cross.

O God,
you willed that your Son be fastened to the
 tree of the cross,
 for our sake,
 in order to deliver us from the power
 of the enemy;
help your chosen people lay hold on the
 grace of the resurrection,
through the same Christ our Lord.
Amen.

May the glorious passion of our Lord Jesus
 Christ
 bring us to the joys of paradise. Amen.

FRIDAY EVENING

*Let us glory in the cross of our Lord Jesus
    Christ,*
*—for in him is our salvation, life and
    resurrection.*

Psalm 130

Ant. Call him Jesus—he will save his
    people from their sins. (Mt 1:21)

In my despair I call to you, Lord.
    Hear my cry, Lord,
    listen to my call for help!
If you kept a record of our sins,
    who could escape being condemned?
But you forgive us,
    so that we should fear you.

I wait eagerly for the Lord's help,
    and in his word I trust.
I wait for the Lord,
    more eagerly than watchmen wait for
        the dawn.

Israel, trust in the Lord,
    because his love is constant,
    and he is always willing to save.
He will save his people Israel
    from all their sins.

Glory to the Father, and to the Son, and to
the Holy Spirit:
as it was in the beginning, is now, and
will be for ever. Amen.

Psalm Prayer

Loving Father of our Savior,
grant that we who are baptized into
the death of Jesus
may die to all sin and selfishness
and be reborn to a life of faith and
service;
we ask this through the same Christ
our Lord.
Amen.

Reading   Gal 2:20

I have been crucified with Christ, and I live
now not with my own life but with the life
of Christ who lives in me. The life I now live
in this body I live in faith: faith in the Son
of God who loved me and who sacrificed
himself for my sake.

Response

Christ was made obedient unto death,
—even death on a cross.

Evening Prayer

Father of mercy,
look upon this family of yours
for which our Lord Jesus Christ did not
hesitate
to hand himself over to sinners
and to undergo the torment of the
cross;
he now lives and reigns with you and
the Holy Spirit,
one God, for ever and ever.
Amen.

Lord's Prayer   **Hail Mary**

*Be a sign of his presence among all men
and bearers of joy.*

Monks of **Taize**

SATURDAY MORNING

Blessed be the name of the Lord,
—now and for ever. Amen.

Psalm 150

Ant.   Glory to God in the church and in
Christ Jesus for ever and ever. Amen.
(Eph 3:21)

Praise God in his temple!
Praise his strength in heaven!
Praise him for the mighty things he has
done!
Praise his supreme greatness!

Praise him with trumpets!
Praise him with harps and lyres!
Praise him with drums and dancing!
Praise him with harps and flutes!
Praise him with cymbals!
Praise him with loud cymbals!
Praise the Lord, all living creatures!
Praise the Lord!

Glory to the Father, and to the Son, and to
the Holy Spirit:
as it was in the beginning, is now, and
will be for ever. Amen.

Psalm Prayer

> Living God,
> may a harmonious chorus of human
>   praise
> blend with the resounding canticles
>   of rejoicing saints
> as we devote ourselves to your honor
>   and glory,
> now and always and for ever and ever.
> Amen.

Reading   Mk 12:29-31

One of the scribes came up and put a question to Jesus, "Which is the first of all the commandments?" Jesus replied, "This is the first: 'Listen, Israel, Yahweh is our God, Yahweh alone, and you must love the Lord your God with all your heart, with all your soul, with all your mind and with all your strength.' The second is this: 'You must love your neighbor as yourself.' There is no commandment greater than these."

Response

> Wake up, sleeper, and rise from the
>   dead,
> —and Christ will shine on you.

Morning Prayer

God our Father,
you teach us to keep all your com-
     mandments
by loving you above all else and our
     neighbor as ourselves;
grant us the grace of single-minded
     devotion to you
and of pure affection for one another;
we ask this through Jesus our Lord.
Amen.

Apostles' Creed   **Lord's Prayer**

*In the twilight of life, God will not judge our
earthly possessions and human success, but
rather on how much we have loved.*
                              St. John of the Cross

SATURDAY EVENING

God is light;
—there is no darkness in him at all.

Psalm 141

Ant. Father, into your hands I commend
my spirit. (Lk 23:46)

I call to you, Lord; help me now!
Listen to me when I call to you.
Receive my prayer as incense,
my uplifted hands as an evening sacrifice.

Lord, place a guard at my mouth,
a sentry at the door of my lips.
Keep me from wanting to do wrong,
or to join evil men in their wickedness.
May I never take part in their feasts!

A good man may punish me and reprimand
me in kindness,
but I will not let an evil man anoint my
head,
because I am always praying against his
evil deeds.
When their rulers are thrown down on
rocky cliffs,

the people will admit that my words
were true.
Like wood that is split and chopped into
bits,
so their bones are scattered at the edge
of the grave.

But I, Lord God, keep trusting in you;
I seek your protection;
don't let me die!
Protect me from the traps they have set
for me,
from the snares of those evildoers.

Psalm Prayer

Heavenly Father,
accept the incense of our repentant
prayer,
blot out our sins
and make us temples of your Holy
Spirit,
that we may watch and pray
for the coming of our Lord Jesus Christ
in glory;
his kingdom will endure for all the
ages of ages.
Amen.

Reading Col 3:1-3

Since you have been brought back to true life with Christ, you must look for the things that are in heaven, where Christ is, sitting at God's right hand. Let your thoughts be on heavenly things, not on the things that are on the earth, because you have died, and now the life you have is hidden with Christ in God.

Response

Our Lord Jesus Christ will come again
    in glory
—to judge the living and the dead.

Evening Prayer

Guard us while we are awake, O Lord,
and keep us while we sleep,
that waking we may watch with
    Christ
and sleeping we may rest in peace;
we ask this through the same Christ
    our Lord.
Amen.

Lord's Prayer   **Hail Mary**

ACKNOWLEDGMENTS

Charles M. Guilbert, Custodian, *Prayers, Thanks-givings and Litanies* (Prayer Book Studies, 25 Standard Book of Common Prayer of the Episcopal Church). For "For the Church," and "To the Holy Spirit."

Community of St. Mary the Virgin, Wantage, England. For "With All My Heart."

Concordia Publishing House. *Good Lord, Where Are You?* by Leslie F. Brandt, © 1967. For "Paraphrase of Psalm 142."

Doubleday & Co., Inc. *I've Met Jesus Christ,* by Michel Quoist, © 1973, translated by J. F. Bernard. For "The Stranger that I Was."

Fortress Press. *Campus Prayers for the '70s,* by John W. Vannorsdall, © 1970. For "For Responsible Decisions," "For Parents in Trouble," "Prayer Before Examinations."

Franciscan Herald Press. *Praises of God.* For "Praises of God."

Geoffrey Chapman Publishing Co. *New Hymns for All Seasons,* by James Quinn. For "Queen of Heaven."

Harper & Row, Publishers. *Prayers for Help and Healing,* by William Barclay, © 1968. For "A Night Prayer."

Helicon Press. *Layman's Daily Missal.* For Acts of Faith, Hope, Charity and Contrition.

Liguori Publications. *Prayers for the Time Being,* by Max Pauli. For "Prayer on a Pencil."

Macmillan Publishing Co., Inc. *The New Testament in Modern English,* by J. B. Phillips, © 1958, 1960, 1972. For Prodigal Son Parable, pages 152-153 in revised edition.

Newman Press. *Tender of Wishes,* by James Carroll, © 1969, the Missionary Society of St. Paul the Apostle in the State of New York. For "Teach Us to Pray."

Paulist Press. *Christopher Prayers for Today,* by Richard Armstrong, © 1972. For "For God's Good Earth," "For Brotherhood," "For a Light in the Darkness."

Paulist Press. *Prayer for Each Day,* by Jose Feder, © 1974, the Missionary Society of St. Paul the Apostle in the State of New York. For "For a Holy Heart," and "For Those We Love."

INDEX OF PRAYERS, PSALMS AND CANTICLES